Display and Publicity
Ideas for Libraries

Display and Publicity Ideas for Libraries

by

Linda Campbell Franklin

McFarland & Company, Inc., Publishers
Jefferson, North Carolina, and London

Also by Linda Campbell Franklin
Library Display Ideas
(244pp., McFarland, 1980)

A companion volume; nothing is
repeated in the present work

Library of Congress Cataloging in Publication Data

Franklin, Linda Campbell.
Display and publicity ideas for libraries.

Bibliography : p.
Includes index.
1. Library exhibits.
2. Public relations — Libraries.
3. Advertising — Libraries.
4. Public libraries — Administration.
I. Title.
Z717.F72   1985   021.7   84-43229

ISBN 0-89950-168-0 (pbk.)

Manufactured in the United States of America

McFarland   Box 611   Jefferson NC 28640

To my whole family this book is dedicated.

Special thanks go to my father, Robert D. Franklin,
for ideas sketched on 3 × 5 cards over many months
and contributed to this book,
and to my mother, Mary Mac Franklin,
for urging us on.

The book is in memory of the
Mermaid of Cossitt Library, Memphis.

Half dried fish, half stuffed monkey,
this 19th century creation drew viewers to Cossitt,
where they were led by a young page, Robert,
into the tower to view her. Whatever part she played
in attracting a more regular patronage, we do not know,
but she stands as a memorable relic
of public relations and display, and as a good family story.
What the mermaid offered to Memphis, libraries offer the world:
mystery, excitement, wonder, and
satisfied curiosity.

Table of Contents

Introduction

This is my second book on display and publicity for libraries. The first book (*Library Display Ideas*, McFarland, 1980) emphasized ideas for school libraries; this one is primarily intended for public librarians. However, in the first book there are scores of tips on lettering, art and craft techniques (including how to make papier-mâché props), and a generic materials shopping list for stocking a display department. Those hints and instructions are not duplicated in this work.

The philosophy that underlies both books is that the librarian's pleasure and duty is to share the library's unlimited riches with absolutely everyone, and that the good fight is to struggle constantly to get people into the library, satisfy them, and make them return. Assured that your product is fabulous, you can use every trick, wile and technique. As ALA President Elizabeth Stone said at the 1982 Midwinter Meeting, "Marketing is selling, not selling out."

A century ago it was said, "Our public may be divided roughly into three classes of reader, — that is, of those who would become readers under more favorable circumstances. The first comprises people of wealth and leisure, together with those who make literature a profession; the second, businessmen of all kinds, who generally can better afford money than time; the third, working men and women, of whom it is no stretch of truth to say that they have neither time nor money at their disposal. The first class can make shift to get on as at present; the second, on the contrary, does not and will not make use, to any extent, of facilities such as we now have, the third cannot if it would.

"The free library must be considered as ... the adjunct and concomitant of the public school, joining in the task of popular instruction even before the latter lays it down, seeking to make permanent results already attained, and to carry on the work of educating people even through their years of maturity."

This appeared in *Scribner's Monthly*, October 1880, in the article "A Free Lending Library for New York." The rich and the literati could use the private Astor and Lenox libraries, businessmen couldn't take the time and in some cases couldn't spend enough money to be allowed to use the Astor

1

or Lenox, and the poor working-class person certainly couldn't gain access. "What wonder, then, that the dime novel and the sensation story-paper pass from hand to hand, and gradually become almost the exclusive reading in thousands of humble homes!" (*ibid.*).

Perhaps we might still describe the situation the same way. The literati and the leisured (as well as characters in search of a chair) already use the library. We need not advertise our wares to them, we need only satisfy their wants. Business people make far too little use of the library, and when they do they don't properly pay for it — with donations or offers to help publicize the library by citing it as their source of information. And finally there are the uninitiated, who don't know of the library's existence and its many offerings. Thousands of these people do read — daily newspapers, magazines, comic books, popular novels, romances, dream and numbers books, and sensational story-papers. This latter category, which we may term the "reading-deprived" class of society, is only part of our target. The third is perhaps the most distressing. This is the "aliterates." In the words of Gene I. Maeroff, writing in *The New York Times*, September 28, 1982: "They are everywhere — people who have the ability to read, but never look between the covers of a book, seldom glance beyond the headlines of a newspaper and search only for the pictures in magazines. Their reading centers around the bare essentials: road signs, labels on food packages, television listings and product instructions.... 'Aliterates' — those who know how to read but won't." He goes on to say that part of the problem may be that people feel no need to read when they can get their information more easily in other ways. He also mentions the Library of Congress' Center for the Book, set up in 1978 to foster reading among people who know how to read, and notes that LC is using television, in part, to promote the Center. TV may be the culprit most easily identified and responsible for most people's belief that all problems can be stated quickly and easily, and that their solutions should and must come within 22–27 minutes, every half hour.

Deep inside, many of us may feel superior because we know the rewards of the library, we have faith in its treasures, and we think that people who deserve to will find their way inside, where they will join the ranks of the privileged. We also know that with so much competition for the attention of the public, we have to do something more active than sit and wait for patrons. We have to get up and shout as loud and convincingly, amusingly and seductively, as anyone else trying to sell something. Plus we have to offer the real goods. This latter point is key to all current discussions of marketing the library, and is as controversial as any matter that faces librarians.

We must align ourselves with, and perhaps even lead the way for, all educational institutions, and cooperate with them to fight aliteracy and illiteracy, or we are all dead. The recent, strong trends to upgrade

Merchandising ... The Genteel Dress Shop Way

SHORT CLASSY NUMBERS LATEST FA...

"This should fit you perfectly, Madam..."

curriculums, and restrict electives and increase emphasis on the 3Rs, are very encouraging for libraries. Perhaps at the brink of extinction, these and other conservation programs will save us.

Barbara Conroy's "Megatrend Marketing: Creating the Library's Future" (*Journal of Library Administration*, v.4, no.4, winter 1983 and collected in *Marketing and the Library*, Gary T. Ford, ed., Haworth Press, 1983), draws on the 1982 book by John Naisbitt, *Megatrends: Ten New Directions Transforming Our Lives* (Warner). Conroy states that "The most pervasive and fundamental pressure from any of the megatrends, of course, is the shift from an industrial to an information age," and goes on to say that businesses "who engage in and market themselves as being in 'the information business'" threaten the very existence of libraries.

Another study by Robert D. Stueart, "Great Expectations: Library and Information Science Education at the Crossroads," in *Library Journal*, October 15, 1981, says that according to a study reported at the Simmons

Merchandising ... The Genteel Restaurant Way

"Our specials today
include, for epigrams..."

College School of Library Service, Boston, 1979, 73 percent of all citizen information needs are personal — solving day-to-day problems, coping with trauma or crisis, news about current events, interest in cultural heritage, religion and family life, and recreation and leisure. "Libraries are listed ninth in their information seeking patterns, with only a small percentage actually using the library, a clear indication that few actually cast the librarian as a diagnostician of information needs." In competition with the librarian in this role are friends and coworkers, crisis center staff and police, newspapers and TV, cultural clubs, ministers, and a stupefying range of entertainment and leisure activity promoters. To be all things to all people, which is what we may be asking the librarian to be, is hard if not impossible. One tactic might be for each librarian to give up or diminish his or her role in areas well served by other community institutions, and to concentrate efforts on what the library can do best. Of course, it's perfectly true that one thing the library does well is combine so many aspects of daily life.

The product you are selling is the well-seasoned *pot au feu* that is an enriched, and constantly changed stew of the experience and wisdom of the ages, world culture, atmosphere, security, adventure and support.

Many of the displays and ideas in this book sell the "feeling"—the massage not the message. Others are meant to catch attention, even steal it from other diversions. These ideas are best used outside the library itself, to get people inside. The various sections of the book are all meant to interconnect and to be browsed for ideas. My intention is to help you learn how to find ideas everywhere about you, just as do fashion designers, pop musicians, artists, and toy manufacturers. Most of you have limited time and or limited space for display and promotion. I say, make time and make space. A rule of thumb used by experts who market things through the mail is "Promote down to the break-even point and you will start making a profit." They mean by this that the larger your target audience, the greater your chance of finding customers will be. And while you must make sure that you know how to reach everyone already in the library—every staffer and every card holder—you must expand your market, and seek always to improve your product.

Versatile Display Elements and Lettering

Handy Holders

3-D props for display cases or windows, or for use on checkout counter or shelf tops. They can be used without any book or sign in a handicrafts display, or to tell about a special new program.

Materials: heavy wire
wood block for base

or

heavy wire
gloves
plastic foam or batting
household glue
wood block for base

or

corrugated cardboard
metal straight-edge
matt knife — good and sharp

Technique: Bend jazzy wire arms and hands from two lengths of wire — the lengths depend on final size, but figure about 54″ for a close-to-lifesize arm and hand. Drive hole in block, or drill — should make tight fit. For the one with gloves, use a short spiral of wire instead of hands, fill gloves with mix of glue and filling material and dry, while on wire spiral.

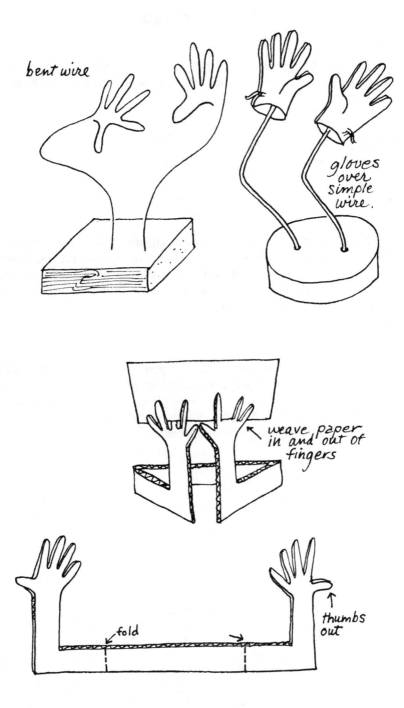

bent wire

gloves
over
simple
wire.

weave paper
in and out of
fingers

fold

thumbs
out

Poster Person

A folding figure to put on cases, shelves or in windows. Make in any size. Can be used for printed or plastic letter messages — on back or chest.

Materials: foam board sheet 4×8
                matt knife
                metal straight edge

Technique: Cut out parts and assemble. You may want to get greater flexibility by cutting legs at hip and knees and taping with paper tape. The upright arm may need some tape to hold in place. Trading left and right arms gives you another position — down instead of up.

Adaptation: Create a miniature of this figure on card stock, printed as a post card or a handout to be cut and assembled, rather like a paper doll, by borrower. It can be a Return the Books reminder, to be put on a table or desk at home, or an announcement for a puppet class.

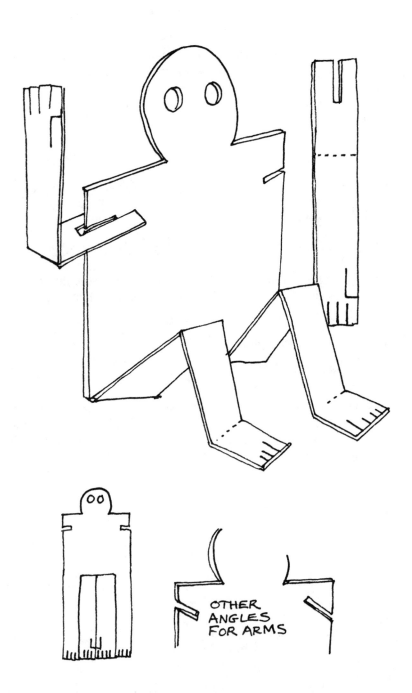

OTHER
ANGLES
FOR ARMS

Outsize Ideas

A sign or poster using an ordinary object blown way up in size, to attract attention. The clip shown here exists, but I can't find out who makes it. However, there is a company making giant paper clips and giant clothespins — Think Big! 390 West Broadway, NYC, NY 10012. Catalog available.

Materials: giant clip
               poster
               message

               or

               flat, cut-out facsimile of giant spring clip, covered with alumi-
                  num foil and shaded and detailed with black permanent
                  marker
               heavy tape
               poster with message

Technique: For latter: cut out simplified spring clip, from foam board or
               heavy corrugated cardboard, wrap with aluminum foil and
               tape on back. Draw details with felt pen, then attach your
               poster with tape on the back. This is not meant to be seen from
               the back.

Tools

Here are some simple, punny signs that can be made to stand alone on a counter or table, or in a case, or which can be made large and hung above various service areas or book sections.

Cut each one out of poster board, after drawing it lightly in pencil. Sketch in the lettering and then finish with a felt pen or glue-on block letters.

Browsing Giraffe Rack

Materials: one 4 × 8 plywood sheet
screws
white glue
tape
spackle
paint
rope for tail

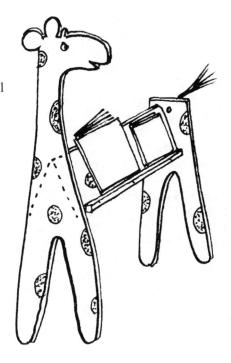

Technique: This children's book rack stands up to 8' high, and is made from one sheet of ½" plywood. It can be built so as to form a double-sided rack for books to be displayed or browsed while standing, or so that books can be read by seated children, one on each side. With a brace underneath the inverted-V rack, the length can be increased to 4' or so. Assemble with glue and screws. If you use very rough grade plywood, splinters will be a problem, so you'll want to "bind off" edges with heavy package tape glued in place, or with heavy rug-binding cloth tape. Spackle knotholes, etc., and paint two coats of background color before adding spots. A menagerie of racks can include a cow, with a rack adapted to have a broad flat shelf top for further display; a lion & lamb combo; a flock of sheep; a pig; or an imaginary bestiary that could be designed by the children. Change rack to "L" to create small desk/carrel.

Etched Lettering

Scotch® Brand Magic Transparent Tape! The poor signmaker's etched glass effect. The only difficult letters are B and D. The B tends to look like an 8 unless the top is made smaller than the bottom. Differentiate a D from an O by slightly canting the top and bottom horizontals.

Lightly draw your words on the outside of the display case or window with a grease pencil. Letters four or five inches high and approximately three inches wide are most suitable for ¾" tape. Apply tape on inside, then clean outside of glass.

Another subtle etched glass effect is obtained by taping a stiff stencil to the glass and temporarily spraying Krylon Dulling Spray on the glass. Dulling Spray is used by photographers to shoot silver.

A third way to get the subtle effect of etching is by using printed acetate tapes. Some color is available, but they are mostly printed in black. Create decorative borders and letters with these tapes, or make fantasy maps or moonscapes with a combination of acetate tapes and topographical sheets. Shading and pattern films, approximately 10½" × 13", are printed in black to suggest waves, herringbones, gravel, sand, woodgrain, etc., and grids, dots and various kinds of lines. A few are shown below. Several companies making printed acetate films are Chartpak, Formatt and Zipatone, and their products may be purchased through artists' supply houses. Matte acetate color sheets make colorful translucent letters or forms, interesting plaids and patterns, and combine with black film.

When trimming acetates and tapes directly on glass, **use a lighthanded approach and do not burnish**. Ask the dealer about a special cutting needle.

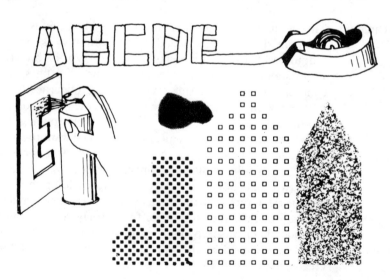

Lettering

Some varieties of 3-D lettering to use in cases or on bulletin board.

Materials: folding ruler and cut-out letters
measuring tape and colored yarn
"screws" of crepe paper or tissue paper

Technique: Arrange initial letters and pin in place with straight pins or pushpins, add supplementary letters. The paper screws are made from 6″ wide strips, preferably 3′ long. Newspaper can be used, along with crepe paper or tissue, but nothing thicker. These letters are easiest to put up by twisting, then pinning top left of each letter, forming and pinning as you go.

Foam Board Figural Letters

To use singly or in combination with displays, or mounted (probably with a block of foam board behind to make them stick out a bit) to bulletin board or back of case. These should be large enough for some detail, which can be drawn on with felt pens, or pasted on after cutting from construction paper. An entire display can be made with small shelves, or hooks in pegboard, with these jaunty letters—or hang them above shelf displays.

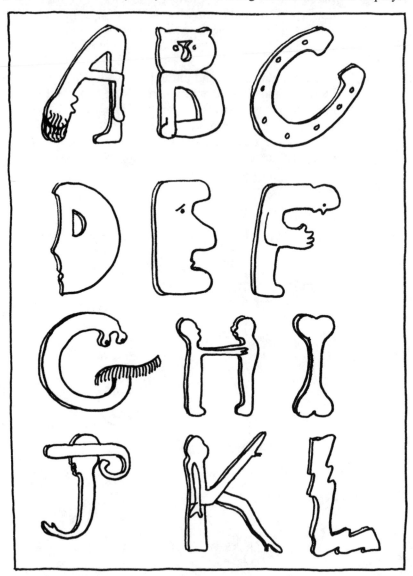

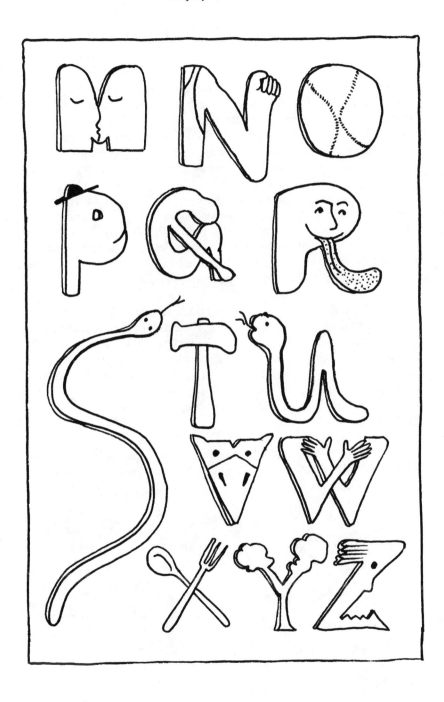

Little Dummy Figures

With some very simple materials you can make a wide variety of small dummy figures for use in displays. Dummy figures of flower girls and attentive spaniels were popular during the 18th and early 19th centuries, and were placed on landings between stairs, or in sitting rooms. Made of thin wood or cardboard, painted or printed in full color, they stood with the aid of easel backs or wooden slotted stands. Make these little dummies the same way.

Picture sources: Draw or trace them yourself, using a fat felt marker, then color; cut from magazines; photostat or photocopy black/white pictures (line art is best) from old books, then color. If the picture is a horse running on a field, cut around the top and sides of horse (and rider), but don't cut away the green grass under its belly or below its feet. You need them for support of the rest of the picture. See sketch.

Stands: Lightweight pictures, say those mounted on file folder card stock, can be made to stand by allowing for a strip of cardboard at the bottom to be bent back, or cut with "teeth" and bent back and forwards alternately. Or, fashion on easel back: this works for lightweight and heavier dummies. Or use a smallish block of wood with a tight-fitting groove cut the length of it, or one or two pieces of photographer's or florist's putty, or — if the picture is small and not especially top-heavy — you can even cut a slot in a big art gum eraser.

These little dummy figures are useful in small spaces and cases, and are just the right size to accompany one book propped up on a desk or counter top — a mini display.

cut away only shaded portion

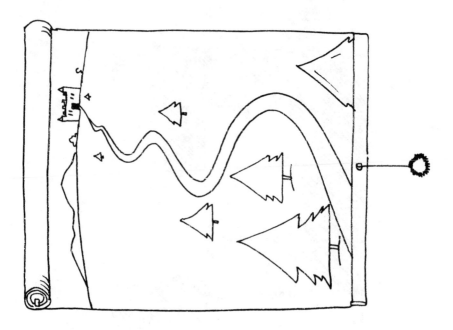

Windowshade Backdrops

Instant pull-down sets for story hours. Can have any kind of theme —
complex or simple.

Materials: window shade, wide as possible
thin colored felt or variety of Con-Tact™ self-stick paper
scissors
household glue and brush

Technique: Pull shade down to length you want. Arrange cut-outs of felt
and affix with brushed-on glue, or use self-stick cut-outs. A
wooden frame for the little shade fixtures has to be built, or
perhaps you can get a shade to fit an existing doorway that
could be blocked during story-telling.

Cat Arches

A doorway decoration, or a freestanding arch for the story-telling room or part of children's room.

Materials: 1 to 4 sheets of foam board
paint (you may want a white cat, or colored cats)
matt knife or sharp knife
wide paper tape

Technique: Draw tall, arched cat on 4 × 8 sheet of foam board, to create an opening at least 6' high. Cut out, then paint or use felt pens to make features, division of legs, whiskers. If you make 3 or 4 cats, they may be assembled to create a little kitty gazebo. Tape on the inside.

Adaptation: Similar arched forms — palm trees, dogs, cranes, draw-bridges, arm-wrestling arms and hands — can be made to use the same way, or in horizontal form to put right up against inside of front glass in case or windows, to create a plane through which objects further back in the window may be seen.

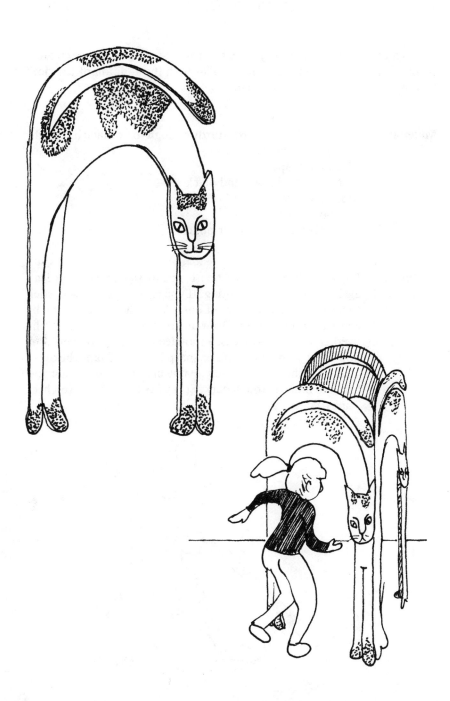

Fairyland Archway

An arch to fasten over doorway. Use for a story-telling room, or create a corner display for winter sports materials — with the addition of the "ice" and the hockey player dummy board.

Materials: 2 sheets of foam board, sturdy enough to be made into arch-
               way and a hockey player
             wide paper tape
             poster paint — brown and black
             wide and narrow paint brushes
             spray-on snow
             mylar plastic sheeting for pond

Technique: Lay 4 × 8 sheets of foam board side by side on floor, or lean against wall to avoid denting. If you crawl on the board, stick to the center that will be cut out, although this means it'll be dented for future uses. Draw an archway of wintry trees, the overhead branches at least a foot deep, making opening 7' off floor. Cut with matt knife or sharp knife, and tape the overhead branches on the back. Paint brown, then use narrow brush to indicate rough bark. Spray fake snow into crotches. Tape to doorway.

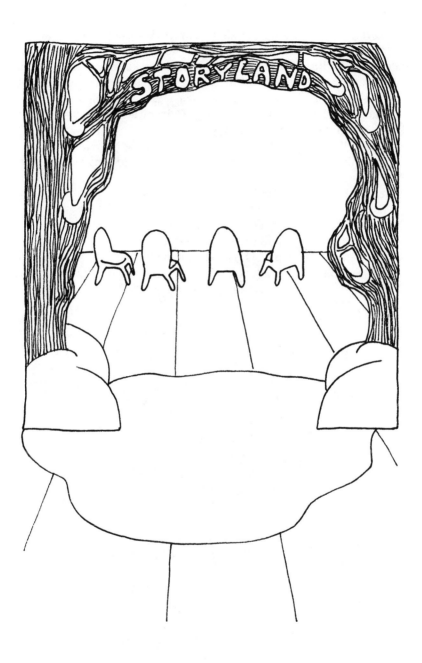

A Star Is Made

After learning to draw a line, a squiggle, a circle, a pyramid, a spiral, a square, and a heart, what a thrill it was to learn to draw a star! And such stars ... created with the kind of control needed for skating on ice or folding a newspaper to be tossed up on a porch. But a star of lines, its skeleton showing the method of its creation, is hard to enlarge for cutting out. Here's a paper star that can be made any size, of practically any paper — from wallpaper to quilted aluminum foil.

1. Fold a square of paper (color or pattern on the outside) in half as shown.
2. Mark edge of A–B in thirds.
3. Fold point C over as shown, then fold ...
4. ... halfway back as shown.
5. Now fold shaded part back again, as shown.
6. Flip remaining double-thickness back under to resemble drawing.
7. Cut as seen on dotted line. This can be a straight-line cut, or zig-zags, or fringe, or scallops. Unfold, and you'll have a pretty fancy pleated star! The steeper the angle of cutting, the more pointed will be the star.

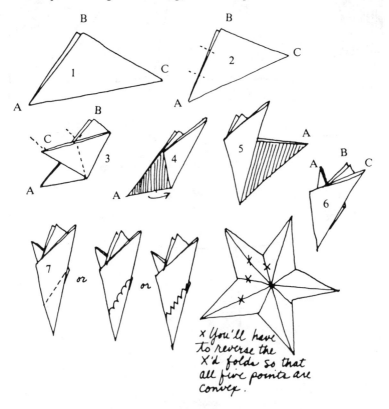

x You'll have to reverse the X'd folds so that all five points are convex.

Using Clip Art Books

"Clip art" is illustration art that has been collected in a sort of workbook and meant to be scissored out and used for whatever purpose you have. There are two kinds, basically: artwork that is free of copyright entanglements because it was done so long ago that copyright laws no longer protect it, and artwork that is free (never copyrighted) because the artists who do it for these clip art books get paid to do that, and may get a royalty on the sale of the book, but no individual fees for the use of the art.

Clip art fills a great need for competent, even splendid illustration, for a very, very low sum of money. An illustrator today, for example, doing a picture of a shoe or a sport coat for a newspaper ad, may get $20 to $35 for one picture. If you need a picture of a very particular shoe or sport coat, you have to hire an artist. If you just need any old shoe, or at least any old high heel shoe, for example, you use clip art. Clip art, particularly antique illustrations from the 18th and 19th century, have had a great effect on the style and appearance of all sorts of printed items ... much more effect than the original artists may ever have dreamed of.

For under $8.00 or so, and often way under that, you may buy a book of collected illustrations, or illustrations done especially for the collection, that may number in the hundreds. In some books, every single picture is different. In others, some pages have the same picture presented in several sizes, to accommodate people with no access to photostatic machines or the new photocopiers that can reduce or enlarge pictures. Almost all of the books are divided up by subject matter, although my favorite by far, and the most versatile and charming book of illustration art you can imagine, is one entitled *Humor, Wit, & Fantasy*, which is the product of Hart Publishing Company, and which was compiled by Pam Pollack. This book is worth its weight in gold, especially for the marvelous fantastical drawings of Jean Ignace Isidore Gérard (1803–1847), better known as Grandville. This French artist may be known to some of you for an edition of La Fontaine's *Fables*. Just one of his illustrations will give you the basis for an entire display, poster or bulletin board. In the context of this book on display, Gene Moore — the wonderful window display artist of Tiffany's, NYC — may be Grandville's closest psychic heir.

27

In my opinion, the new art should be used sparingly in your productions. Particularly the illustrations of humans, which look very outdated quickly. It is due to some mysterious glamor of the ancient, perhaps, that a figure drawn in 1830 somehow looks more lively and pertinent than does one drawn just three or four years ago — at least in commercial illustration.

The Hart Picture Series is, as a whole, better produced than any of the others. The glossy paper aids the photocopying or photostatic processes, and the selections seem more imaginative. The Dover Pictorial Archives Series is quite good, and a selection of their books will offer up just about any illustration you may need. At one time there were nearly 50 or so titles available. Now it seems to be down to about 20 or fewer. I understand that Dover maintains a sort of "day old bread" outlet for O.P. and damaged books down on Varick Street in NYC, for any of you planning a trip to the Big Apple.

One marvelous book is unusual because it was first collected and published in 1886. It has been beautifully reproduced, and should be in any general art collection, where the display person can consult it. That is Tuer's *1,000 Quaint Cuts.*

For modern drawings, there are a number of companies offering books of clip art, perhaps most notable and widely available are those in the Dover Clip-Art Series™ and the Formost Self-Adhesive Clip Art Series of Graphic Products Corporation. The latter is enticingly easy to use, with stickum on the back of each page. Just clip it and stick into place on the mechanical for the printer. (A mechanical is the "board" — actually heavy card stock — on which a page is laid out in final form for the camera, and on which type, lines, pagination and illustrations are stuck in place.)

Primarily for Antique Illustrations

Hart Picture Archives

The Animal Kingdom. Compiled by Pam Pollack. NY: Hart Publishing Co., 1977. 399 pp, sources for illustrations given.

Goods & Merchandise. Hart Picture Archives. Compiled by Robert Sietsema. NYC: Hart Publishing Co., 1978. 127pp, sources.

Humor, Wit, & Fantasy. Compiled by Pam Pollack, under general editorship of Harold H. Hart. NYC: Hart Publishing Co., 1976. 430pp, sources.

Weather. An Engrossing Collection of Over 200 Pictures in the Public Domain, Which Can Be Used Without Fee or Permission. Compiled by Pam Pollack. NYC: Hart Publishing Co., 1977. 96pp, sources.

Dover Pictorial Archives

American Bird Engravings. All 103 Plates from American Ornithology by Alexander Wilson (1766–1813). NYC: Dover. 102pp + xix.

American Indian Design & Decoration. By LeRoy H. Appleton. NYC: Dover, 1950, 1971. 277pp, with sources and many pages of myths and folklore.

An Old-Fashioned Christmas in Illustration & Decoration. Edited by Clarence P. Hornung. 2nd enlarged edition, with over 250 illustrations. NYC: Dover, 1975. 153pp, sources. *Note:* Mr. Hornung, a commercial artist of great standing, has been a designer for at least 50 years, and many of his designs — for posters in WWII and other things — would be recognized by you. He has a personal collection of enormous size of ephemera and illustration, from which this book is drawn.

Animals. 1419 Copyright-Free Illustrations of Mammals, Birds, Fish, Insects, Etc. A Pictorial Archives from Nineteenth-Century Sources. Selected by Jim Harter. NYC: Dover, 1979. 283pp.

Art Deco Designs and Motifs. Over 100 Examples. Rendered by Marcia Loeb. NYC: Dover, 1972. *Note:* This is a collection of contemporary renderings of designs from the Twenties. Almost exclusively geometric, without figurals.

Banners, Ribbons & Scrolls. An Archive for Artists & Designers. 503 Copyright-Free Designs. Edited by Carol Belanger Grafton. NYC: Dover, 1983. 94pp.

Children. A Pictorial Archive from Nineteenth-Century Sources. 240 Copyright-Free Illustrations for Artists & Designers. Selected by Carol Belanger Grafton. NYC: Dover, 1978. 118pp.

Decorative Alphabets and Initials. 123 Plates — 91 Complete Alphabets — 3,924 Initials. Copyright-Free for Artists & Designers. Edited by Alexander Nesbitt. NYC: Dover, 1959. 123pp, sources.

1800 Woodcuts by Thomas Bewick and His School. Edited by Blanche Cirker. NYC: Dover, 1962. 247pp, sources. Bewick (1752–1828) revived the great art of fine wood engraving. His natural history illustrations may be his best known.

Food and Drink. A Pictorial Archive from Nineteenth-Century Sources. Selected by Jim Harter. NYC: Dover, 1979. 139pp.

Goods and Merchandise. A Cornucopia of Nineteenth-Century Cuts. Compiled and arranged by William Rowe. NYC: Dover, 1982. 60pp, many illustrations crammed in amusing ways on each page, no sources given.

Harter's Picture Archive for Collage and Illustration. Over 300 Nineteenth-Century Cuts. Edited by Jim Harter. NYC: Dover, 1978. 91pp, with an interesting essay on creating a collage of old illustrations.

Quaint Cuts in the Chapbook Style by Joseph Crawhall (1821–1896).

Selected and arranged by Theodore Menten. NYC: Dover, 1974. 88pp. (The collage in this book with two people in stocks comes, in part, from this clip book.)

Treasury of Art Nouveau Design & Ornament. A Pictorial Archive of 577 Illustrations. Selected by Carol Belanger Grafton. NYC: Dover, 1980. 137pp, sources & artists.

Treasury of Victorian Printers' Frames, Ornaments and Initials. Edited by Carol Belanger Grafton. NYC: Dover, 1984. 123pp.

Art Direction Book Co.

1,000 Quaint Cuts from Books of Other Days Including Amusing Illustrations from Children's Story Books, Fables, Chap-books, Etc., Etc.... London: Field & Tuer, The Leadenhall Press, ...; NYC: Scribner & Welford, 1886. Reprint edition: NYC: Art Direction Book Co., 1973. (19 W. 44th, NYC 10036)

For Contemporary, Recently-Drawn Art

Dover Clip-Art Series

Food & Drink Spot Illustrations. Designed by Susan Gaber.
Ready for Use Borders. Designed by Ted Menten.
Silhouette Spot Illustrations. Designed by Bob Censoni. NYC: Dover.
Illustrations of Children. Designed by Tom Tierney. NYC: Dover.
Illustrations of Hands. Designed by Tom Tierney. NYC: Dover.
Illustrations of Women's Heads. Designed by Tom Tierney. NYC: Dover.
Sports Illustrations. Designed by David Carlson. NYC: Dover.

Formost Self-Adhesive

Travel, School Days, Leisure Time, Home & Family, Special Times, Borders & Panels. Rolling Mills, IL: Graphic Products Corporation, 1981. Each title about 30pp.

Collages with Clip Art

First, in my opinion, it's better to sacrifice a tiny percentage of reproduction quality and keep your clip art books intact. *Don't* clip out the art you want to use, photocopy it and then cut it out of the photocopy.

Illustration collages can be used as blown-up backgrounds for window or case displays; for posters; to decorate the pages of annual reports or reading list brochures; as the focal point for a bulletin board; or as logos for library signage or publications.

The ideal collage is much more than the sum of its parts. It takes advantage of the broad spectrum of subjects, and the varying sizes, and allows us to move time and space around, to alter perspective, scale, context and sizes to create new dimensions.

Illustration collages are useful for visual puns (see the Eli Kince book in the Bibliography at the end of this book), and in that way help us show the pubic how the seemingly disparate parts of the library's collection add up as a fascinating unit.

Just playing with two or three images, putting them into different relationships with one another, acts to stimulate the imagination. It's rather like a childhood game that my librarian father played with my brother and me. We all would name something to be a character, then Daddy would make up a story about the three things. Once a garden hose was the featured character. Unrelated animate and inaminate things from the clip art books suggest stories and worlds of almost mythic quality.

Essential Tools & Equipment

A photocopying machine, fine paper scissors, and a glue stick are all you need to get started. The photocopying machine must make good, clear, clean copies, not slimy gray ones with smudges and streaks. You may have to take your clip art books to a photocopying shop if you don't have a good enough machine. In fact, such a shop may provide you with a further useful tool: one of the new machines that can reduce or enlarge images.

Photostatic reproductions are a further tool. They are extremely clear, and are made on glossy, heavy paper like photographic print paper, and they can be made with great accuracy in a wide range of sizes. Blueprint shops can also blow up images or reduce them, and blueprints are a lovely color.

How to Put Images Together

Until you get used to the techniques, it's best to make your photocopies, then carefully and closely cut around each image, right up to

the line. For the first stage, leave in such things as long
shadow lines cast by the figure or object, as these may
be wanted in the final collage.

Overlapping is the easiest way to join images; cutting and slitting and weaving are other techniques. To
make flying saucer disappear into someone's mouth,
you may be able to fit the edge of the flying saucer
image over the open mouth in such a way to look as if
it is either coming out or going in. A close-
mouthed image may have to have its mouth slit
along the line between upper and lower lips to fit
an edge of the flying saucer in between. More ex-
treme is the technique used so successfully and
hilariously by Terry Gilliam, the artist who did
the animated illustration collages that introduced
parts of the famed Monty Python Show from
England, now seen on late night TV. Gilliam
would cut along the lip line and down the chin-
defining lines, then — through the magic of animation — the chin would appear to move up and
down, à la Charlie McCarthy, to emit sounds

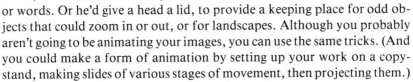

or words. Or he'd give a head a lid, to provide a keeping place for odd objects that could zoom in or out, or for landscapes. Although you probably
aren't going to be animating your images, you can use the same tricks. (And
you could make a form of animation by setting up your work on a copy-
stand, making slides of various stages of movement, then projecting them.)

Don't try to put too many elements together at first. It gets awfully
complicated. A visual pun can successfully be made with just two disparate
elements — disparate as to size, subject or relationship in the real world. Arrange and rearrange on a plain piece of paper until you're satisfied. Then,
to do the final assembly, tape pieces together on their backs, then use a glue
stick or little "wraparounds" of tape to affix the images to the paper
background. Now you can choose to photocopy this collage, which will be
twice (and in some cases, thrice) removed from the original in the clip art
book, or have it photostated. It can stay the same size or be made larger or
smaller, or you can make multiples to use in one place or on several related
displays.

Sometimes — as with my opening books "the hard way" collage (see
page 42), the tin can on the right — you have to add something in ink. There,
I cut the can lid, moved it into an open position, then drew the missing
curved line of the can's edge.

Recreating Famous Pictures ... with a Twist

If you can think of a collage to try, practice by redoing a famous painting. Three good ones are Michaelangelo's Sistine Chapel creation, with Adam; Leonardo daVinci's Mona Lisa; and Rousseau's Sleeping Gypsy.

(1) Find images of figures with outstretched arms, some clouds and a book. Create a collage that shows one hand giving a book to the other, against a cloud background. Maybe it's for a display on weather books.

(2) Find images of a broad landscape, a large woman's head, and something in the shape of a smile — a cucumber, say, or a canoe — and replace the mouth with one of them. What does this mean? Why is she smiling? You think up something, and add a book to tell your point.

(3) Find a lion and a moon image, put on a tan paper background, and let the lion look down at something odd, that's striped like the gypsy's coat.

Adding Other Elements

Clip art is in black and white. You can print on colored paper, or color all or part of your collage. Or add some images cut from colored magazine pictures. These contemporary images are under copyright, so do not plan to use a modern image reproduced in a library publication. For a window display, bulletin board, or posters around the library, it would be okay. Another element to add is 3-dimensions — by pasting collages on sides of cardboard boxes. You can virtually build a building by pasting architectural images or columns on all sides of a box or carton.

Add words. Some of the best and most useful words, and readable typefaces, are found in newspaper headlines. Keep a file of unusual juxtapositions of words for future use. Sports pages often have some of the best in the whole newspaper.

Presenting the Collage

You will want to think about how you want it to look on the page or the poster. You can put it in a frame or border. In fact, some clip art books are nothing but frames and borders. Or let the images float on the page's space. Framed is more formal and precise-looking, and the illustration is really set off from the text. Floating — or "silhouetting" — the image on a page is less formal, somewhat more modern looking. It is an attractive technique because type can be made to fit around the edges of the picture. If you plan to use your typewriter for the text, lay the image on the page, sketch light pencil marks around it to guide your typing, type the copy to fit, then glue or tape the picture in place. You may have to type it twice to make it come out.

The possibilities are as endless as the combinations are infinite. Once you get the illustration collage habit, you may never want to stop!

Clip Art Compositions

The following are all poster or bulletin board ideas that can be adapted to use as a graphic background in a case or window display. Any special notes are given below.

Listen to Reason. Made up of two pictures — man with headset and wires attached to 4 books (cut from a picture of 5). Scale can be altered. One use is for display of recorded books. "Talking Books" is a protected name, initiated by the Library of Congress in 1931. Another headline: "Why Not Listen to a Book?"

A Good Head. Seated figure silhouetted from background, his right arm cut at elbow and bent over belly to hold another cut-out, the book. Three more pieces of art — the books creating the head — were trimmed and fitted together. Can be used without legend.

Dreams Come True. Imp is from one picture, and was cut to fit into box. Use for display of fairy tales or books on dreams. Another headline: "Surprise!"

Playing Geopolitics. Two images — the boy and a globe, which replaces bubble in original. "The World's a Great Place for Play," or, in a more serious vein, "Don't Blow It."

Spice to Life. A short cruet bottle replaced with books — note that they're the same as the books in "Listen to Reason." New labels or spines for books could be doctored to make into cookbooks, mysteries, etc.

Dig In. The same overt message as the one above — books are appetizing, so is learning. Can be used without head.

Santa's Gift List. This doesn't represent a collage of clip art, but a way of taking part of an illustration to make a verbal point. This Thomas Nast Santa is very well-known.

Reading Is Fun. Humor is somehow easier to achieve with the old linecuts. Here 2 unfortunates in stocks, one of which was not holding anything in his upraised hand, are given humor by the addition of an outsize book. Could be used for word game events, displays on using the dictionary to avoid misunderstandings, the latest novel in great demand, or could be coupled with a suggestion to share a book by reading aloud!

Opening a Book. First, to show you how the preceding were constructed, here's one made up of 5 elements. Note how the can lid was "opened" and the can rim drawn in. This one could go without the head too. It's a hard habit to break — the habit of verbalizing everything. Store windows, particularly the spiffier clothing boutiques, show us how effective visuals can be without words.

PLAYING GEOPOLITICS:
A Film Series at the Library

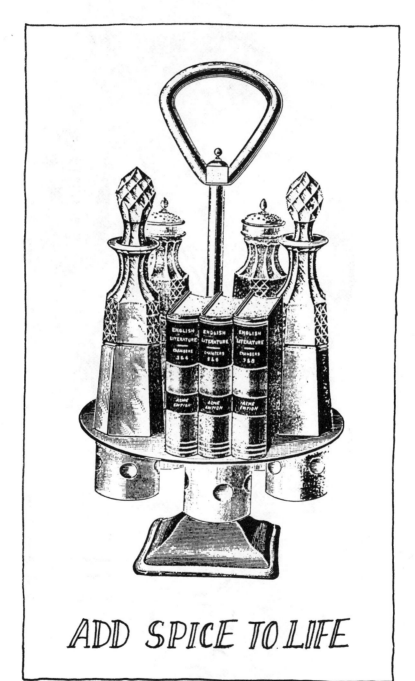

ADD SPICE TO LIFE

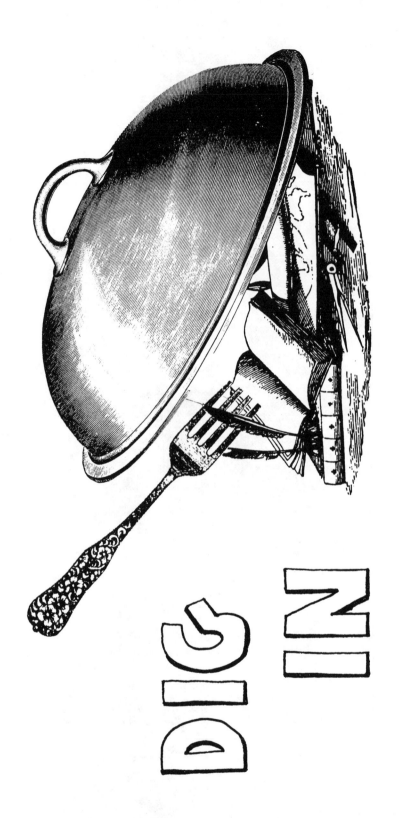

What If Santa Couldn't Read?

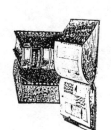

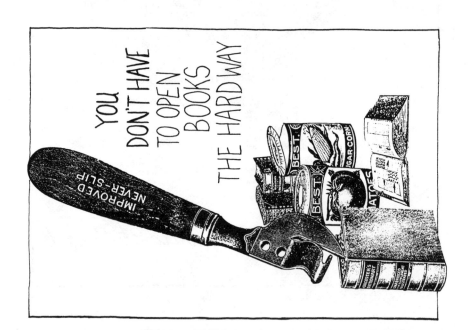

YOU
DON'T HAVE
TO OPEN
BOOKS
THE HARD WAY

Services and Book Care

Library Bond Issue

Poster, and graphics to use on other advertising for building fund or bond issue. Can be made up into 3-D display with a model library building of cardboard, manikin hands or gloves, coins or paper money.

Materials: light blue background poster board
red paper for building, to draw bricks on, or as is
tan paper for hands
black masking tape to create windows
plastic wrap for windows
foil for coins
permanent felt marker
plastic lettering

Technique: Cut out simple building that represents library. Cut out windows and tape plastic wrap behind holes. Cut narrow strips of black tape to create window frame. Cut out hands and coins. Arrange on poster board, add details such as crack in edifice, columns and a door. You can use masthead from library stationery over door. Add headline message and foil discs for coins. A permanent marker will draw on foil.

We Worry (About Overdue Books)

Poster or bulletin board, or little ad campaign in newspaper, or flyer to send
out with overdue notices.

Materials: Dark poster board
               paper to cut out librarian and the chair and the books on shelf
               paper for sidewalk and sign outside, plus plastic wrap to tape
                  over it for glass
               narrow black masking tape
               small printed calendar
               marker to write headline

Technique: Draw librarian and chair (you can simplify this mightily by
               making the chair with its back to the viewer and only the head
               and gripping hands of the librarian visible). Position but do
               not glue on poster board. Assemble simple elements of side-
               walk and sign and glue together, then glue in place on poster.
               Tape piece of plastic wrap taut over it, then glue librarian in
               place. Glue on calendar, and add shelf of books. Use plastic
               lettering or marker to create headline and message.

Overdue Books

Reminder, to send out with all notices, about overdue books. Some libraries in the country have resorted to drastic measures — large fines, arrest and jail sentences. You can hardly blame them — books belong to the whole community and keeping them amounts to petty larceny. Amnesty programs seem to enjoy great success.

Materials: calendar pages
red poster board
plastic lettering
black felt pen

Technique: Arrange overlapping calendar pages, add lettering. Accompany with smaller versions, photocopied on red paper, to mail out, and to insert in all borrowed books.

THE YEARS
PASS QUICKLY...

DO YOU HAVE SOME
OLD LIBRARY BOOKS?
DON'T SELL THEM AT A YARD SALE, OR
GIVE THEM TO A THRIFT SHOP! YOU
CAN RETURN THEM ALL, PENALTY
FREE, ALL THIS MONTH & NEXT.

FROM 1980 ....185 books still out
FROM 1981 290
FROM 1982...1764
FROM 1983...2119
FROM 1984...1940
FROM 1985..1730

Overdue Books

Easel-back countertop display for the library, classroom, any place where people who may have library books will see it. Even local restaurants might put one on the checkout desk.

Materials: corrugated cardboard or foam board
               thinner cardboard
               household glue
               felt markers

Technique: Cut out sign, anywhere from 1½′ long to 6″ long. Draw hand like the hand used to return letters to sender. (Clip art books abound with such hands.) Glue on easel back that will allow it to rest nearly upright and hold under pressure until completely dry.

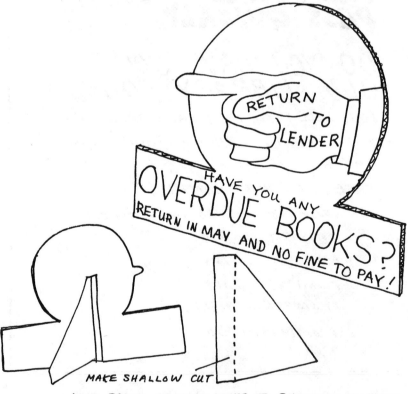

MAKE SHALLOW CUT
WITH RAZOR OR MAT KNIFE TO SIMPLIFY FOLDING.

Keep the Waves Down ...
Don't Rock the Books

or

We Welcome Walkmans When Walkmans Whisper

If indeed you allow patrons to wear earphone radios (as long as they cannot be heard by anyone more than a foot away), then let them know. Many people—especially those who listen to music while reading at home—will appreciate your policy.

You might try a bookmark with the words "We Welcome Walkmans & Other Sshhhh Earphone Players ... but keep 'em muffled, please. This library allows radio and tape players—but only if only you can hear them."

Or you might try pushing your record collection by saying "Tape from our wide variety of records—then you can Travel to Traviata, Read to Ravel, Meditate to Mendelssohn or just Grin to Grand Master Flash!"

Or in a small display window, put several books, wearing earphones borrowed from a local shop for a week, along with your rules.

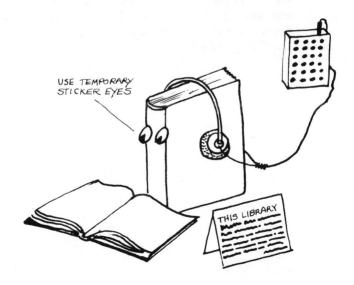

Don't Get Wet

Case display, poster or small counter display near checkout (where you might be selling plastic shopping bags) to encourage protection of books from rain or snow.

Materials: one or a pair of men's rubber boots or galoshes, and one or a
                    pair of women's
               2 or 4 books to fit down in
               marbles, gravel, baker's pellets to weight boots
               umbrella
               fish line for hanging umbrella
               "puddles" made from clear varnish or plastic wrap
               sign lettering (optional)

Technique: Weight the galoshes so that they will stand up when books are
               tucked in tops. Suspend umbrella over them. Create puddles
               and put up lettering. Actually, the lettering really isn't
               necessary. Include a plastic book bag, tacked to the back of
               the display, or leave as is.

Bookmobile Summers

Make the bookmobile a more inviting, restful and comfortable branch by adding awnings and a few chairs. In summer, advertise fewer but longer stops and invite people to sit and read a while — magazines would be good. Have people bring chairs, or provide a few stools.

Materials: gaffer's or duct tape
2 or 3 fittingly printed shower curtains
4 metal poles or large pushbroom handles
mallet
heavy rubber bands

Technique: Tape together 2 or 3 shower curtains to arrange over top of bookmobile and hang over as awning, or tape 2 directly to sides. Pound poles into ground, and use wide, heavy rubber bands to secure curtains to poles. Set up a banner, and a couple of chairs. If the sun is really hot, you may not want to tape to car roof — it might end up damaging the finish. Use bricks or concrete blocks.

Bookmobile Schedule

A printed flyer to announce establishment of bookmobile schedule and services.

Materials: colored offset paper
             paper cutter

Technique: The effectiveness of this piece depends on the way the top
             looks after the flyer is folded. Some offset printers cannot
             handle such a job—their paper cutters aren't the right kind,
             so they say. Work out what kind of camera-ready mechani-
             cals you need, with the printer. You can do a more elaborate
             piece with an 11 × 17 sheet, folded 5 times.

Adaptation: Using sheets of foam board, you can create a free-standing
             display screen or bulletin board.

Lend a Helping Hand

A counter display to show what the library can lend to help, or to advertise specific types or titles of books.

Materials: real manikin hand or glove hand *or*
              cut-out cardboard hand
              circulation card and pocket, with card typed on with "title" —
              "Helping Hand"
              strong doublefaced tape
              any pile of books

Technique: Use strong tape to attach pocket to hand. If the hand is old, the finish may be flaky or chipped, in which case you might want to fasten the pocket on with a bracelet of some kind. Position hand over books.

Borrow a Friend

Poster to advertise a "mutual friends" program, where library assists people of like interests to share some time together. This can be set up so that everyone who joins the program is really volunteering to be a friend, not revealing a friendless state.

Materials: poster board
              paper for cut-out figures — 2 colors
              plastic lettering

Technique: Draw simplified outline of walking person, and smaller stand-
              ing person to fit under arm. Assemble, arrange and paste in
              place. Add lettering, which can also be done with felt pen.

Adaptation: A small bookmark/flyer to be inserted in one book checked
              out by each borrower can be created by using the simplified
              standing figure, cutting the arms up so that it fits over page
              edge, and printing on stiffer paper than 50-pound offset.

Spotting Opportunities

Poster or bulletin board, or adaptable to very small case display. Advertising job counseling program.

Materials: white poster board
                black construction paper
                white pencil or grease marker
                black felt marker
                red felt marker
                plastic letters
                doubleface tape or paste

Technique: Cut out dominoes and die with the rules of perspective in mind so that they will be more dramatic graphically. For the black dominoes, draw white border and the dots. Cut out the dot/holes if you like, and leave off borders. Mark dots on die. Attach to poster board and add lettering.

Raise Your Sights

Poster or bulletin board to advertise lending program of various optical instruments, and or film showings on biology, astronomy, bird-watching.

Materials: poster board
               clear plastic sheeting
               colored ink, catsup, thin paint
               white cardboard for slide
               color photo from magazine
               transparent tape
               lettering

Technique: Cut two pieces of plastic sheeting, slightly in perspective to create dimension. Put small blob of ink/paint/catsup between layers, mush a bit. Tape slide to poster board. Sandwich colored picture between two photo-slide shaped cut-outs of cardboard. Tape to background, overlapping or slightly under other slide. Add lettering.

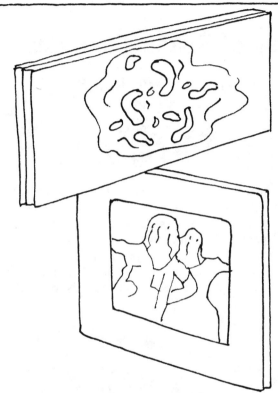

IMPROVE YOUR SIGHT
THE LIBRARY LENDS
· MICROSCOPES
· SLIDE & MOVIE PROJECTORS
· TELESCOPES
· BINOCULARS
· OPERA GLASSES
· BOOKS TO HELP
(BOOKS FREE ; MACHINES REQUIRE SMALL DEPOSIT)

Promotion of Reading and Learning

Books I Have Read

A booklet about $5\frac{1}{2} \times 4\frac{1}{4}$, 16–32 pages, made with stiff paper covers and stapled binding. These booklets can be made with different covers, and should be sold rather than given away — for $1.00 or less.

The pages can be prepared on a typewriter. Type AUTHOR   TITLE NOTES   DATE READ at the top, with underlining above and under. Then type .... dotted lines, doublespaced, all the way across the page, leaving a ¾″ margin left, right, top and bottom. At the bottom right of recto pages, bottom left of verso pages, put a small linecut of a book or bookish subject, taken from a clip art book. Make a countertop display, and use the slogan "Someday you'll wish you had a list of all the books you've read!"

Libraries: Handy Things to Have Around

Poster, or cut-outs to tape to inside of front glass of case, maybe with a few books seen through them in the case. Use for crafts or "Helping Hands" display.

Materials: colored paper to cut out figures, hands and books — different
            colors or all the same color, or black and white
          lettering to apply to case or onto poster
          thick felt pen
          poster board, if desired

Technique: Cut out very simplified books, running figures and similar shaped hands, as depicted. Each can be simply outlined with felt marker. Arrange elements with a sort of pattern in mind, but with elements rather widely separated. (Or make them very dense either at top or bottom, and thin out at other end.) Add lettering and books, if desired.

Online Database Searching

3-D freestanding display that can be made any size, for countertop or floor. Use for advertising computer catalog search services; print on brochures about library's computer system.

Materials: foam board (4×8 sheet if large figure is to be made)
blue poster paint
gold paint for buttons
felt markers to do face
wood for stanchion and dummy board base
red, white, black paint for stop sign

Technique: Cut out policeman figure (or policewoman) and paint. Cut out stop sign and letter. Make dummy-board base. You can make one with 3 or 4 slotted pieces for versatile placement of future dummy boards. Paint like sidewalk or cobbles or grass.

Other
Heads: **Stop Computer Literacy**
Look Both Ways ... You Are Sure to Find a Book You Like

STOP

DESKTOP

DUMMY BOARD PLAT-
FORM FOR MIX &
MATCH WITH
VARIOUS FIGURES

Sentencing

Any size dummy board, the smaller the more versatile, for use as a sort of mascot. A 6″–10″ figure can be put right on bookshelves, on checkout desk, in windows and cases.

Materials: foam board
                   paint or felt markers

Technique: Cut out judge and his high desk, make wood dummy board
                   stand, and color and letter form.

WE'LL HELP
YOU GET
SHORT AND LONG
SENTENCES
IN STORIES, NOVELS,
BIOGRAPHIES, HISTORIES,
MYSTERIES, POEMS, ETC.

Find Out by Nosing Around

Display prop for small case with reference books.

Materials: cardboard cylinder, which can be a Quaker Oats box or a cylinder made up from very stiff cardboard and taped.
paint
sharp knife
plastic 3-D lettering

Technique: Cut out nose profiles, and push out from within. Paint with poster paint or spray paint. Add lettering. For mobile, bend wire into nose. Other noses can be created by collaging many, many noses cut from magazine pictures and pasted on a disc or a large nose-shaped piece of cardboard.

bent
wire
mobile

cut profile and
bend out

Race Your Engines

Poster or 3-D display to advertise general pleasure and stimulation of reading.

Materials: *For Poster*
                green poster board
                red paper for car/book
                black paper for wheels
                gray roadway paper
                paper for flag, driver and chain of spectators

                For 3-D Display
                green background paper
                gray roadway paper
                fat, tall but narrow book, such as a pocket travel guide
                bright red or British racing green shiny paper or paint
                toy/doll driver
                toy wheels

Technique: Cut out and assemble parts for poster, add lettering. Or create
                a race car from a book, by putting striped glossy paper cover
                on and resting on wheels and adding doll's head and arm. In
                fact, several books done up this way would look great.

Let a New Book Race Your Engine!

Roosting in the Library

A poster or bulletin board to encourage the use of wide variety of collection's books.

Materials: tan poster board
              red-brown construction paper
              white paper
              yellow felt markers
              straw or dry grass/weeds
              black felt markers
              foot square of chicken wire
              piece of faded calico or grain sack

Technique: Cut out smallish window at top for fox. Tape chicken wire up
              on back. Cut out fox's head from red-brown paper, and white
              chickens from white paper. Paste to board. Add paper cut-
              outs of books, draw on generic titles. Sketch woodgrain on
              board of coop. Add "grain sack" (which can also be made
              from a piece of light-colored, small-flowered wallpaper).

Stack Up on Books

Display case, adaptable to poster, to give a practical solution to the home bookcase problem: where do I put another book! If you borrow them, you can return them.

Materials: table with sawed off legs
              chair with sawed off legs
              stacks of books
              lettering for front of glass

              and

              real chair
              floor lamp or desk lamp
              stacks of books
              plastic lettering

Technique: In a case you can put the table and chair with short legs, stacked with books. In a tall case or window, put a chair and an area rug and a huge stack of books, and light with lamp. This is a great display to leave on late at night, perhaps on a timer to go off at midnight. Add a bookmark of a stack of books, the reverse side to tell about some of odder collections available for borrowing, or a pitch to get a library card.

Other Head: **Booked to Capacity**

Terry Belanger, of the American Printing History Association, reported the following tale, which gave me the idea for this display: Once a visitor to Samuel Clemens asked why he felt it was necessary to have books all over the floor, tables, chairs, and all other flat surfaces. "Well, you see, it's so hard to borrow bookcases," was the answer!

Three-Dog-Night Reading

Poster or bulletin board, adaptable to a case display or countertop display, for wintertime, bedtime reading.

Materials: blue poster board
brown, red, white, yellow papers to use for the dogs
tan Kraft paper for person
red paper for book cover
felt marker for lettering

Technique: Cut out dogs from different papers, draw details on. Cut out person and book and hands. Paste down in position, then draw blanket line and person's features. Add lettering, which may be a combination of drawn letters, cut-out letters or plastic 3-D lettering. Add book jackets, or facsimile book-shaped elements with names of books printed on them.

Adaptation: Use a blanket, pillow, huge book, 3 stuffed dog toys and lettering for a case. Or baste together 3 stuffed dogs and tie to cardboard sign: "Get a good book to read in bed." Put this on the counter near checkout.

Lunchtime Reading

Case display, mainly to set mood and show how nice it is to have a book to read. You can even make a small scale case of acrylic sheets, in which to create a variety of room settings for book readers.

Materials: tension poles for curtains, to fit case or window
cloth for curtains, or real cafe curtains
sawed-off table and chair
paper for menu
checkered tablecloth
tape to create lettering in window

Technique: Place sawed off table in window, with chair. Put tablecloth on, hang curtains — probably on 3 sides, with back side blocked off with paper, although curtains all the way around would be intriguing. Menu can be printed up — a booklist, perhaps divided into "Appetizers," "Main Courses," "Nuts."

Adaptation: For a simple shelf display, use a placemat, fork and spoon and either the reading menu, or a featured book.

LUNCH READING

Saw legs off old chair for case or window.

MENU
Main Entrees

lunch.
Reading
Appetizers

Desserts

Soups

Print up a "menu" book list. Draw a tassel and border around typed titles.

Reading in Bed

A mood-setting case display, which can be made very very small with a doll and doll bed.

Materials: curtain tension poles
             long curtains
             colorful sheet or blanket
             pillow
             pajamas
             pillow head
             stuffed glove for hand
             good bedtime reading book

Technique: Hang curtains and create the bed using anything puffy under
             the sheet. Stuff pajamas and attached glove, and put in
             pillowcase head with drawn on features. Add lighting from
             corner looking down on book in narrow spot, if possible. This
             one works best if you can see only part of the reading figure —
             hang curtains all the way around, or at least sheer curtains to
             soften view.

Adaptation: Create a very small version with a doll of any kind and a doll
             bed, curtains and a miniature book.

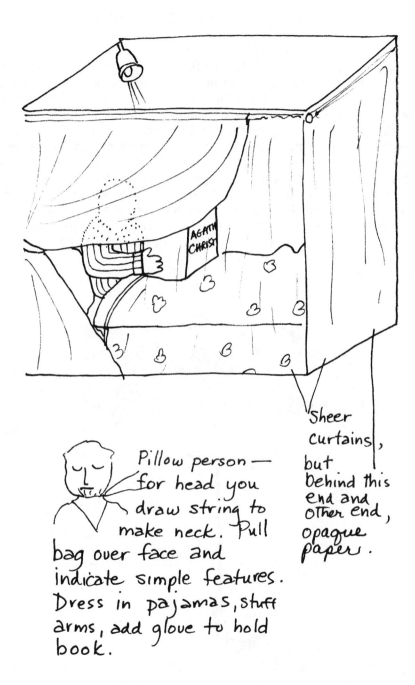

AGATH CHRIST

Pillow person —
for head you
draw string to
make neck. Pull
bag over face and
indicate simple features.
Dress in pajamas, stuff
arms, add glove to hold
book.

Sheer
curtains,
but
behind this
end and
other end,
opaque
paper.

For Full News Coverage ...

One way to get a new patronage into the library might be to advertise the newspaper reading room. Take an unloved umbrella from Lost and Found, open it and wire it open. It may have been lost because it kept closing up around the owner's head. Using a 2″ paintbrush, coat one section at a time with white household glue. Cover with a front page from one of the newspapers you subscribe to. With one hand underneath, and one on top, smooth and press the newspaper into place. Wash and dry hands, then do the next section. When finished, neaten up your work by touching up corners and trimming edge. Paint the shaft, if you like. Suspend over a display of newspapers and news magazines in an outside window, or inside the front door. Put one up at the Courthouse, a barber shop, a town meeting hall. Make a few, paint the motto in red, and get people in rain gear to pass out flyers on corners around town.

Balanced Diet

"SIT DOWN WITH A SERIAL TODAY ... it might bowl you over!" Mount photocopies of first pages of various serial publications to the fronts of real cereal boxes. Display with a cereal bowl and spoon, or coffee cup, on a checkered tablecloth. Offer a wide variety or two or three addressing the same subject from different angles. If serials are hard to find in your library (and they often seem to be down winding steps and long corridors), provide a map to encourage readers. Usually the trouble with pushing serials is the patron's lack of awareness, a timidity about using the materials. You might try a once-a-week (at different times) orientation talk on using indexes and online database accessing. Some alternate headlines: **"Get a Good Start on Your Day,"** or **"A Serial Can Fill You with Facts."**

The Library as a Newsstand

Shallow 3-D display or bulletin board to show wide variety of periodicals available.

Materials: black background paper
striped paper for awning
Kraft paper for newsvendor
felt pen to make features
lengths of corrugated cardboard to create division of racks
staple gun
magazines or just magazine covers
newspapers

Technique: Starting with background paper, build layers, stapling as you go — the awning, the newsvendor, the back rack, then 3 magazines, the next rack over their bottoms, and more magazines, and so forth. Add a sign band — "Ask inside" — then do newspapers, then bottom of stand with rest of information.

Additional: Bookmark done up like simplified version of the newsstand, plus information on range of materials available to see at the library and those which can be checked out and taken home.

USE STAPLE GUN TO
AFFIX THREE LAYERS
OF MAGAZINES &
CORRUGATED CARDBOARD
STRIPS TO BACK OF
DISPLAY WINDOW.

Dead Letters

Poster, or small element in display, about letter collections. This can also be used for local history letter collections. Create a booklist to hand out.

Materials: poster board
               envelope
               red sealing wax
               aluminum foil
               cardboard
               household glue
               letters or felt markers

Technique: Paste envelope on angle, and put blob of sealing wax, or draw one with thick red crayon. Cut simple letter opener from stiff card stock or cardboard, and cover with aluminum foil. Leave some of the cardboard exposed on the back so that it can be glued to envelope. Add lettering.

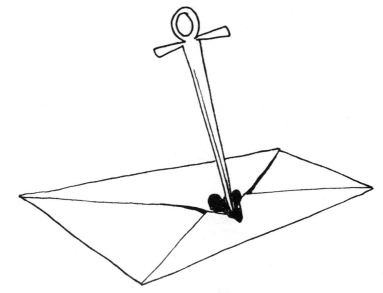

"B" Is for Book

B is for Bibliographies, Biographies too. Poster or bulletin board, or adaptable for hanging display. Just an attention getter — no specific message.

Materials: background poster board, light blue
white paper for book pages
yellow and white paper for book covers
paper or plastic flower
pink narrow satin ribbon 6″ long
plastic letters

Technique: Cut out elements of books and paste down, inserting piece of pink ribbon as proboscis for bee-books. Glue down flower and add lettering and the stripe effect of the ring or spiral binding with felt markers.

Adaptation: Using nylon fishing line or thread, open books can be suspended in flying position. Pages of the books may have to be taped together, only slightly fanned. Hang over a pot of real mums.

is for Books

Redecorate with Books

3-D case or window display, or poster or bulletin board, if made from flat cut-outs. General advertising of the value of using the library.

Materials: at least 6 old books which can be painted, one of which should be big and flat for a carpet, one small for a mirror or picture frame
2-sided tape
paint in "decorator" colors for the books. To coordinate. Use decorating magazine for latest fashion colors
small flower vase and artificial flowers or dramatic cactus
picture of a carpet or rug large enough for big flat book
plastic letters

Technique: Painting may warp the books and make them hang open and wrinkled. Tape pages or tie narrow band of string to hold tightly closed for painting (you can do touchups later). If you feel ambitious, the desk/table books can be painted like faux wood or marble, or just in brown or some color. Coordinate the book "screen" and frame. Arrange and add letters.

Wired to Learn: Artificial Intelligence

Case or window display, adaptable to bulletin board. To advertise computer books, online database services, books on robotics.

Materials: lots of colored wires, circuits, resistors, capacitors, used in
                  electronics
              modern chair
              fishing line
              lettering
              book(s)

Technique: Create brain, spine and limbs of a humanoid from the wires,
              circuits, etc. Set figure on chair, wire head and upraised hands
              from ceiling. Attach pages from book, or newspaper. Put up
              lettering and book(s).

Adaptation: To create bulletin board or poster—use real wires and small
              colorful circuitry hardware and staple to posterboard
              background. Use cut-out paper chair and letter with felt pen
              or use plastic lettering.

Buried at the Dump?

Poster or bulletin board, done collage technique with simple overlap, or 3-D case display. They may be used simply to pose a question, or to provide a partial answer.

Materials: shades of brown and tan paper
cut-out paper TV
tin can pictures cut from magazines
heavy felt pen

or

cut-out books, of red and blue
angular alphabet letters
paste

Technique: Assemble layer by layer, from the sky through succeeding planes. Or cut large tan Kraft paper wasteland and draw a few drift lines with felt pen, then cut along top of those lines and insert cut-outs of TV and cans or books and alphabet letters.

Adaptation: For 3-D display, rest old TV or large books at angle securely on cartons, then fill the case part way with crumpled paper, packing materials, obvious waste.

WHITHER TV?

ARE BOOKS DEAD?

TV or books rest on boxes; rest of the space filled in with crumpled trash paper.

Brown or gray paper front of case (or front and sides)

Social Issues

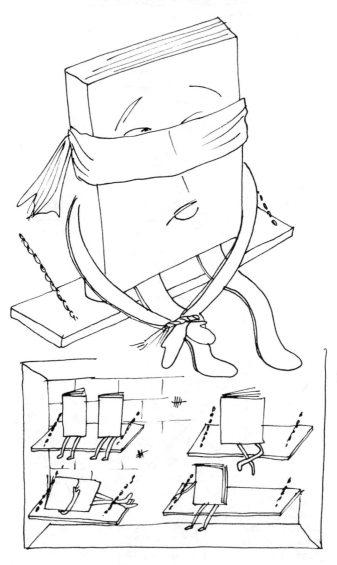

Censorship of Books

This idea came from an unsigned drawing in the *New York Times* in 1984, accompanying a blurb about an exhibition at the Rare Book and Special Collections Division of the Library of Congress, called "Hidden America: Suppressed, Censored and Privately Circulated Books." (The drawings below and opposite are the author's.)

This would be most effective done as a wall display, or with a fake wall that could be built and set up in the central court. A dungeon wall, painted battleship gray with lines to delineate the stones or concrete blocks, plus graffiti—perhaps, as in the drawing (which I cannot reproduce for you), scratched off days. The books can be made from cartons, and painted with woebegone faces. Legs and arms can be made of cardboard too. One book should have a ball and chain (make one with a black bowling ball and a very heavy, black-painted chain) and the other should have its hands tied together and a cloth gag tied around its "face."

You could also build a small bed, hung from the wall with chains, that the books could sit on.

If you do this as a small case display, make one wall of the case the wall of the prison, and build several chain-hung beds, with book prisoners.

The display can feature famous suppressed books, books threatened in some school systems and library systems, or be an effective way to ask the question of your patrons: *"Should we lock knowledge up and throw away the key?"* or *"What kind of sentence would you give a book you don't agree with?"*

Shocking Ideas

The reaction is electric — when you start thinking. Poster or bulletin board, adaptable to shallow case display. It's its own message — no product beyond ideas to sell.

Materials: blue poster board
             aqua poster board or construction paper
             brown paper for diving board
             frosty paper or side of milk jug, for light bulb
             masking tape
             strong, clear doubleface tape
             yellow marker and black permanent marker

Technique: Cut out all elements, including the light bulb from the flattest part of the jug. Use doubleface clear tape to hold light bulb in place. Put aqua water on, draw water, pool edge, lettering, and light bulb's legs and arms and eyes. Put masking tape over end of light bulb and color yellow.

Adaptation: With a heavy enough piece of cardboard, like thin corrugated board, you can make a diving board, the tip wrapped in strips of red cloth tape, and use Crazy Glue to add real light bulb, with pipecleaner legs.

Pigeonholes Are for the Birds

Poster or bulletin board to show how books can help you fly the coop, or cooped up feeling. Can be adapted to case display using a Christmas season 3-D dove figure.

Materials: blue poster board
              16 squares of corrugated cardboard
              matt knife
              white and gray paper for pigeons
              black paper
              lettering
              felt marker
              facsimile book (a James Fenimore Cooper?)
              straw
              cardboard wooden blocks

Technique: Cut holes in each of 15 squares. Tape cut-out pigeon heads
              and straw in place and add black paper behind. Glue in place,
              leaving place for 16th square, into which you create a burst-
              out hole, with straw and black background. Cut out full
              pigeon and book. Add headline, although it is not necessary.

Is It Fun to Be Different?

Shallow case display, or shelf. The appeal of being yourself, following your own bent, your own path.

Materials: 10 to 15 gray or black shoes, left and right, all same style and
              color but different sizes, plus one red shoe, very jolly
              crepe paper and google eyes
              pegboard back and shelves
              a few books
              another pair of google eyes
              card for credit

Technique: Select background color, then put up shelves. Arrange shoes borrowed from shoe store, all facing same direction, looking somewhat bored. At bottom, or on another shelf, put the gay red shoe with your added crepe paper bow and google eyes. (Don't glue or tape, and make sure the paper color won't run on shoes.) You may want to borrow the red shoe from a staff person. Glue other google eyes on watcher. Add credit line for shoe store, and selected books.

Red Tape

Case or window display of any size, even miniature, for library materials and books intended to assist people in dealing with bureacracies.

Materials: as much red hem binding as needed to crisscross case you use
               at least 7 times: anywhere from 7 feet for small case to 30
               feet for large case
               suction cup hooks or transparent tape
               scissors, or clear photocopy of large shears
               background paper if desired (color should set off red tape)

Technique: Use crazy cat's cradle idea and put up crisscross red tape,
               back and forth. If you have the tape or binding, or if you want
               to use the much less expensive acrylic yarn, certainly the more
               intricate the crisscross the better. Set up books and lay
               scissors near them, or temporarily fasten sections of the
               scissors photocopy, cut out, to the book covers.

Adaptation: Set up a small double shelf of interesting but little-used books
               in a window. Use gray thread back and forth like a sloppy
               spider web from the books to front of case. Add spider.

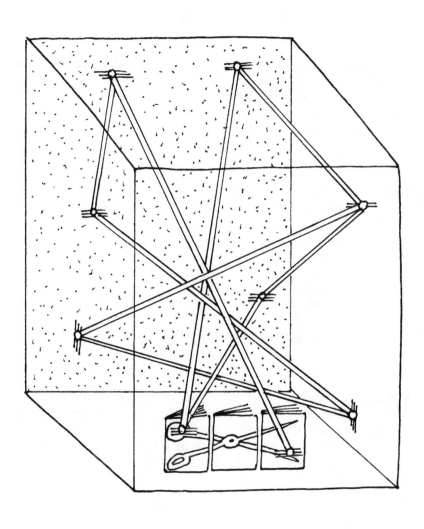

TOP VIEW

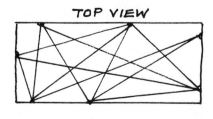

Alone or Together

Shallow case display or bulletin board — primarily mood setters. On top, the person alone has book(s) for company — the book can be upbeat and fun, or could be on subject of making friends, surviving divorce, whatever. On bottom, a person with a book comes along to meet someone seated at table. Book can be on a variety of subjects.

Materials: chair and table (can be small-scale, like children"s folding table and chair, as long as they don't look like children's furniture)
   strong background color paper
   hat
   gloves
   books(s)
   nylon fishing line
   wigs
   (or all paper cut-outs for bulletin board)

Technique: Arrange setting as shown in drawings. Two keys to success are the strength and simplicity of the arrangement, and dramatic lighting, if possible to arrange. I don't often speak of lighting because I realize how difficult it may be to arrange "fancy" spots and other lighting fixtures that can be moved.

You've Got the World in Your Hands

3-D display prop to use in pushing books on various "worlds" and the Earth's environment.

Materials: background paper — color dependent on chosen "world"
               tan construction paper (2 sheets 8½ × 11)
               brown and black felt pens
               variety of colored poster boards or large sheets of paper
               double-sided tape or paper glue
               one paper doily (for woman's cuff)

               or

               piece of corrugated cardboard, with corrugations showing on
                  one side (for cuff)

Technique: Choose the world as baseball during baseball season; as egg;
               as mirror; the world as a microscopic view of bacteria; a sky
               full of stars, seen through a telescope; a dissected circle; the
               world as a globe; the world as a percentage pie. Select colored
               paper for this world and cut a 16″ to 20″ circle from it. Draw
               details: baseball stitching; crack in the "egg" and a chick's
               head; paramecia and odd leggy germs; stars and a planet; a
               statistician's pie, etc. Cut out two hands, making sure that if
               the paper has a wrong and right side, the hands are a left and a
               right. Draw fingernails. Glue hands on background on either
               side of the "world." Put a drop of glue, or small piece of
               double-sided tape, on the tips of two fingers, and lightly curl
               the hands around and touching the globe. Cut out cuffs and
               glue or tape in place.

Adaptation: Use several small hands, cut from various colors of pink, tan
              and brown paper, and do a display (or a poster) on the theme
              We've All Got the World in Our Hands or **It Belongs to Us
              All** or **We've Got the Whole World in Our Hands.**

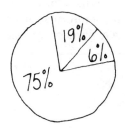

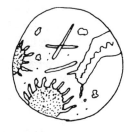

Trace your own or a child's hand.

Dead Drunk

Small case display, tabletop display if made with glue, poster or bulletin board if made with paper cut-outs. Use euphemism to make message.

Materials: 2 toy cars & toy trees from railroad model
hammer
bits of broken glass
charcoal gray paper for roadway or broad strip of coarse sandpaper
green paper
plastic letters

Technique: Create roadway with the gray paper. Glue down to green paper ground and add trees. Crush cars with hammer, and arrange on roadway, or against trees. Sprinkle broken glass. Add lettering, or books on alcoholism, or information on AA meeting at the library, or a pile of AA flyers or info sheets.

Family Farm

Poster for series on the future of the family farm.

Materials: blue & green poster board   paper to create farm and cow
                    banker's blue or gray paper   felt pen, black
                    burlap Con-Tact® paper   plastic lettering

Technique: Cut out man, sack, farm, clouds if you like. Attach green to blue poster board — not quite at the halfway point. Paste banker in place, add lettering.

Displays and Bulletin Boards for Specific and Miscellaneous Subjects

Sports and Games

Catch 'Em at the Library

Poster or bulletin board for the baseball season; current best- or hot-sellers; easily adapted by changing small book-ball into cassette, reel, picture of book on specific subject.

Materials: background paper, light blue and green
brown Kraft paper, tee-shirt paper, vest and glove paper, white paper
felt markers for wire mask, delineation of vest and features
headline letters

Technique: Put the green grass paper down over blue poster board. Cut out face, and arms from Kraft paper; cut glove and vest from other shades of brown paper; glue all in place; draw mask in wide felt-tip pen. Cut out little book, or use clip art picture of one. It should be white like baseball.

Adaptation: A small case display can be made with a catcher's mitt nestling a book or other library item. Or have made up into tee-shirts.

Runner's Poster

Poster or bulletin board to use with books on running, or books that help
you become a winner, or books on physical fitness.

Materials: poster board, medium gray
              black acrylic or poster paint
              running shoes with good tread
              yellow paper tape
              window screen
              toothbrush
              felt pens, red and black

Technique: Use toothbrush dipped in paint loose enough to splatter, and
              rub on screen to create spatter effect on gray poster board. Put
              yellow stripe in place at diagonal. Put running shoe in puddle
              of semi-dry black paint and make footprints — probably you
              should make first one on newspaper, then 2nd on poster. Do
              same for other shoe. If you don't have shoes with good tread,
              approximate the tread with felt pen. Add headline in red.

Other Head: **Prepare for the Race** which can be figurative — preparing for
              the future, for a career.

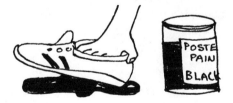

Tackle the Heavy Ones

Football season; this can be fall for schools or beginning of new year after the bowl games. "Hard" books. Poster or bulletin board.

Materials: blue or green poster board
black or dark brown felt marker
colored paper for uniform, helmet, skin
book jacket or book-shaped sign with names of some "hard books"
paste or doubleface tape

Technique: Cut out football player of Kraft paper or of colored paper (be careful if you are a public library not to use the school colors of only one school), paste or tape to background. Draw simplified details, including the word "LIBRARY" on front of shirt. Paste or tape up book jacket or book substitute, add hand over it. Draw lettering lightly with pencil, then mark. Add grass line.

Other
Heads: **Get It and Run With It**
Don't Let Books Get You Down: Tackle Them
Touchdowns in Life's Games — Books Help

Books to Charm

Books on manners, romance novels, white magic, magician's tricks, charming glimpses of the past. To hang over bookcase.

Materials: a sheet of foam board (many brand names — see materials appendix) large enough for the size arm you want — I suggest making it quite outrageously outsize
felt tip pens — broad nib — black and red
foot-length or so of brass chain from hardware store. The kind used to hang chandeliers
string or fishing line to string
piece of cloth to gather and staple as sleeve end

Technique: Cut out long forearm and hand with pointing forefinger. Cut out 3 or more books. Draw lines to delineate fingers and edge of arm — on both sides (remember the fingers show nails on the palm side), and lines to show books' pages. Gather and fold and staple cloth all the way around the elbow end. Fasten books to chain, chain around wrist, and hang so that hand end is slightly low.

Abracadabra!

Poster or bulletin board, adaptable as 3-D case display. Could be books on magic; better to be unusual or unexpected materials available at library.

Materials: shocking pink poster board
                black construction paper
                white paper or real glove
                black felt markers
                plastic lettering
                black stick or artist's brush handle
                book jacket or substitute book

Technique: Cut out top hat and sleeve from black paper. Fix in place with white cuff and glove (if you use a real glove, staple in place). The wand can be the same as the baton used in another display with a conductor. Insert book jacket, or dummy book with a subject written on its cover. Add lettering.

Related
Event: See if you can get a party magician to donate time (in exchange for publicity and exposure to potential customers) and do a magic show where he/she pulls magical things off bookshelves, and miniature books from behind people's ears, etc.

Pursuing Trivia

Poster to advertise reference services that can help people win the game!
You might persuade game stores to enclose a flyer with every game they sell.

Materials: poster board
              paper to cut out for figures
              felt pen for lettering, or plastic lettering

Technique: Cut out simple figures, stools and game table, arrange and
              paste to poster board. Add letters. Make up booklist of
              reference books that would be of value to players of the
              various types of Trivial Pursuit™ games, in different subject
              areas – from sports to movies.

Money and Investment
Fiscal Fitness

A bulletin board or poster, with attached flyers, to advertise books on financial planning.

Materials: light green poster board   photocopied flyers
                dark green felt marker   heavy duty stapler

Technique: Draw simplified view of part of a greenback, with Washington holding a barbell. Staple on flyers. Add lettering.

Other   **Give Your Money More Muscle**
Heads: **Is the Dollar's Strength Good?**
              Strengthen Your Assets

Books Into Money

Poster on how to turn booklearning into financial rewards or books on how to start a business or increase profits or whatever. Use to promote library book sales.

Materials: black poster board
              play money
              dustjackets or facsimiles
              corrugated cardboard to create the machine and rollers
              paper to cut out arm and hand
              black and red markers
              plastic lettering
              household glue or paste

Technique: Cut out cardboard struts for money-making press, also rollers and gears (which can be discs on which you ink the teeth). Glue the back part of the press, the conveyor belt, and the bottom roller to poster board; then glue one by one a joined strip of play money, and the books on the conveyor belt, then the top roller and the nearmost strut. Add arm and hand, and shiny red handle, then the lettering. As with many displays, often the point is made without words.

Monetary Cycles

Poster or bulletin board for lecture series or display of investment books. Use at year's end, when people are planning finances for tax reasons.

Materials: light green poster board
aluminum foil
corrugated cardboard, or stiff card
tape
permanent marker: a "Sharpie®" will mark on just about everything, including metal foil
household glue
green construction paper or play money

Technique: Cut out corrugated cardboard discs—a drinking glass and a luncheon plate are good templates to draw the circles. You can use a very sharp kitchen knife, or a safety razor or matt knife to "saw" out the discs. Use to cut out slightly larger circles of aluminum foil—there should be enough margin to fold over edge of cardboard, and tape in place. Use blobs of household glue to affix discs, glue on money for bike's body. Draw simplified coin images, including serrated edges. Draw or use black masking tape, cut narrow, to create handlebars.

Vested Interests

A case or window display that can keep the same headline through several simple changes. Many librarians have little time, and welcome a display that can be changed in short order. (1) business vests, dollar signs, books on financial investments; (2) bulletproof vest(s), police shield, books on hand-gun laws, law enforcement profession; (3) ethnic costume vests, national flags, books on folk customs; (4) down vests, skis, books on winter sports; (5) hunter's vest, decoys and duck stamps, book on wildlife conservation.

Materials: vests
               coathangers
               nails
               colored or black tape to create symbols on front glass
               various props and books

Technique: Against background hang vests on nails. On front glass make tape dollar signs, police shield, etc., place books and other objects on floor of case, or on boxes covered with paper to match background paper.

We'll Suit You to a T

Window, case or display over shelves, to attract attention with neat tee-shirts, and to encourage reading. If kids were encouraged to work at a design with clever wording for their own tee- or sweatshirts, they might go on to other creative uses of language.

Materials: clothesline
               several tee-shirts with slogans (including baby tees)
               coat hangers for each
               clothespins for each
               heavy cardboard or scrap of foam board
               books
               felt pen

Technique: String clothesline, hang up colorful array of tee-shirts. Cut out cardboard tee-shirt, bigger or much smaller than real ones, make easel back for it, and letter. Put in a thank-you card for loaners of the shirts.

Adaptation: Cut out a tee-shirt chain for use as border decoration. Or have each child make such a 6–10 shirt chain and create a cartoon strip on it, or a lengthy greeting card, or a simple message.

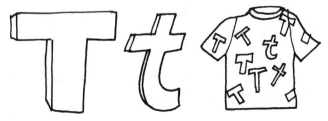

cut tee-shirt "chains" to paste in rows on poster or bulletin board. Put one letter (or word) on each shirt to spell out message.

Tin Cans

Row of cans, labels removed, spray-painted appropriate color, playing on word "can"—with film can. Or a row of cans, labels removed, with a book with idea of "can" in title, headline: "YES, YOU CAN":

Or a row of tuna fish cans, label on, with book on fishing and a huge cutout fish hanging above:

Or cans for which you've created special purpose labels—perhaps photostated large and small for hugest can you can find and smallest. Contrast size and/or contents.

Back to School

Poster for adult education. To advertise career and education counseling.

Materials: poster board — yellow
             brown wood-like Con-Tact™
             several pages of white paper to create book
             paper for sleeve, hand
             real pencil
             lettering

Technique: Cut out student's chair armrest, paste to poster board. Staple
             3 sheets of 11 × 17 paper and fold to create "book." Glue or
             tape to desk top and write in message. Add arm and hand, and
             glue pencil in place. Add lettering.

Thinksgiving Celebration

A poster or bulletin board to promote books and learning at holiday time, or some unexpected time of year. Motto can be used for bookmarks and for booklists or flyers. Do cooperatively and set up posters at bookshops, or have a book sale with booksellers' booths midway between Thanksgiving and Christmas.

Materials: colored background paper — green or bright yellow or brown
              Kraft paper for the turkeys
              crayons or colored felt pens — browns, oranges, reds, yel-
                 lows — to color birds
              cut-out book, with or without title
              plastic lettering

Technique: Cut out large turkeys and paste to background, except for
              turkey's "hand," which must be holding a book cut-out. Add
              lettering.

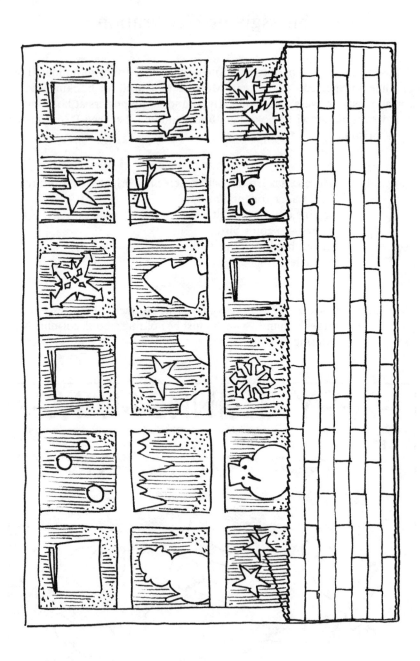

Happy Holidays!

Christmas or middle of winter (adaptable to Halloween, Thanksgiving, Fourth of July); to exhibit pertinent books for the season. Display case, window. Adaptable for bulletin board.

Materials: black masking tape
manila paper or newsprint or construction paper
corrugated paper printed with bricks, a roll of it. Or red wrapping paper drawn on with felt pens to suggest bricks. Blue background paper
books for the season
spray snow

Technique: On inside of glass, lay out the windows of a classroom with masking tape. Fasten brick paper inside — across the front, or around 3 sides. In a case display, you'll need the back "wall" of the room papered over. Spray Jack Frost on the individual panes. Add paper cutouts, either done as children would do them, or in a very sophisticated way to contrast. Add books or jackets. No headline needed.

Three-by-Three Windows

Window displays, for two or three adjoining windows, or for dividing up a long bulletin board. One is 3-D, the other uses flat cut-outs. The idea is to continue from one window to the next, not to have separate entities.

Materials: (1) doll dressed as queen
long train of cloth or paper
toy train tracks
large cut-out paper letters or drawn or plastic letters

(2) ladders — can be made of icecream sticks
toy babies or angels or cherubs, or pipe cleaner figures
small painted shelves
pegboard backing

(3) flexible plastic or cloth tubing over wire frame
colorful paint
papier-mâché for head
wire tongue

Technique: Assemble parts, making sure that the continuous element leaves one window and enters the next at the same point. You can add books and or words. The serpent with polkadots, for example, might pop out of his hole and see either a book or a message on the side wall facing him.

Right on Target

Case or window display, adaptable for poster or bulletin board, to draw attention to just about any kind of materials—books on the far right in politics, books on archery, books on the theme "There are a hundred ways to miss a bull's-eye, and only one way to hit it."

Materials: paper tape
              suction cup arrow
              books and bookstands

Technique: Trace large circle, which doesn't have to be in center of glass, on outside of glass. From inside, carefully stick concentric rings of black masking tape or red tape. Stick arrow up, after moistening inside of suction cup slightly. Prop up books. You don't need a headline. You could also stick up the printed paper targets used at target galleries. These are much smaller, and you may want to trim around circle, or put up several.

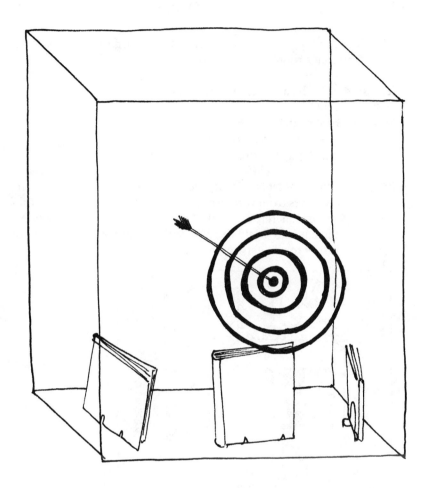

Back board of case can be
painted a color, or covered with
a collage of cut-out leaves.
Use black or colored tape to
create the target on inside of
glass. You can make clear vinyl
jackets for books — also with targets.

Totem Poles

Freestanding display, to add to each week as a record of some goal being reached. Children's room or for adults.

Materials: milk, bleach, cider plastic jugs
                      cans
                      broomstick or other pole
                      heavy wood base or concrete base
                      paint, paper, wire

Technique: Cut, assemble, paint, decorate with button eyes, etc., creatures from variety of jugs. The base must be heavy: thick wood, concrete or metal. If concrete, you can pour ready-mix cement into tin lid of large canister, and insert wooden pole just before it gets too hard.

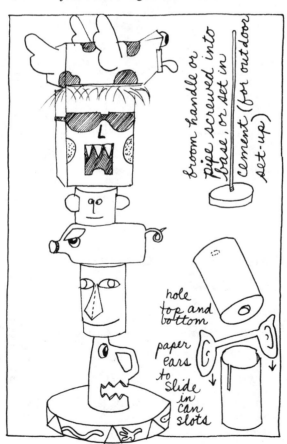

Helicopter Ideas

3-D display, to hang in small case or over shelves. Speaks for itself on bright ideas, or use for electrical inventors.

Materials: light bulbs
                striped drinking straw
                discs cut from sides of plastic milk jug
                nylon fishing line
                permanent black marker
                transparent tape

Technique: Tape length of fishing line to light bulb — you'll need strong but clear tape. Use the clear tape used for shipping packages, to cover address labels, for real strength. Thread on ⅓ to ½ drinking straw, then disc of plastic for the rotors. Hang. If you use against a background, make it blue, with white clouds, and add lettering if you like.

... At the End of the Tunnel

Small case display, done as a series so that you only have to change the book and one object suspended in front of the tunnel. The idea of doing continuous series might be a good way to pique the interest of occasional visitors, turning them into frequent visitors.

Materials: large diameter accordianing tube, of plastic over wire rings
             dark background paper and floor paper
             objects: **light** bulb, **sight** glasses, **height** ruler, **knight** chess-
                 piece, **fight** boxing gloves, **mite** cut-out bug, **blight** dead
                 plant, **flight** toy airplane, **bite** false teeth or computer part,
                 kite small kite, **write** big pencil or toy typewriter.

Technique: Arrange large tunnel-tube so that it snakes around a bit.
             Fasten one end up a few inches on side of case, after putting
             up dark background (black good). Hang working light bulb
             in front and add book. Hang or set other representative ob-
             jects for successive displays.

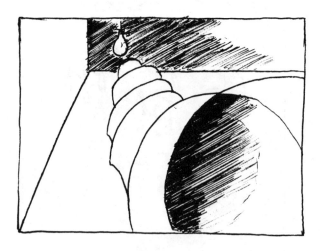

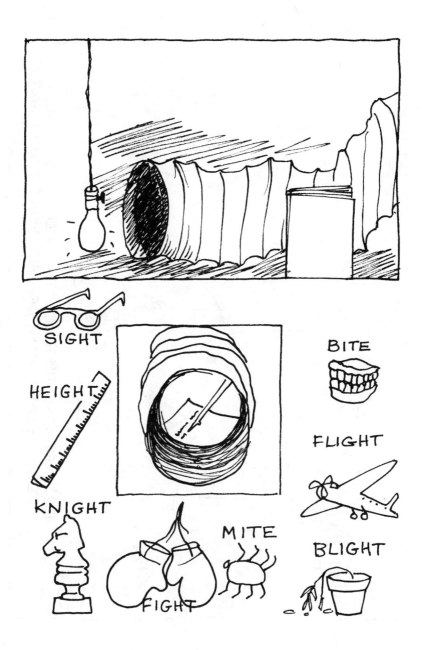

SIGHT

BITE

HEIGHT

FLIGHT

KNIGHT

MITE

FIGHT

BLIGHT

Rube Goldberg Inventions

Bulletin board or poster, could be — if you've lots of patience — made into a case display.

Materials: colored paper for cut-outs
                 sandpaper
                 real match
                 lettering

                 or

                 toy frog
                 match
                 toy car
                 candle
                 bent clotheshanger
                 toy saucepan
                 toy watering can

Technique: Cut out shapes, assemble and paste to poster board.

Adaptation: Planning-sketches of this kind of thing, along with descriptions of how they work, and what they will do, are the most fun. Have kids and adults participate.

The Arts

Famous Art Revised

This case or window display, which makes full use of the front plane instead of ignoring it, is to attract attention to one book or library material further in the case. Can also be done on glass in a picture frame, and hung in front of a display on the wall.

Materials: heavy white grease pencil

or

narrow white masking tape

or

white acrylic paint and narrow artist's brush

tan Kraft paper
deep blue background paper
striped towel or bathrobe

Technique: Tape poster you are copying or adapting on inside of window or case, and follow major outlines with grease pencil, tape or brushed-on paint. Or adapt without poster and alter spatial relationship of objects. Put in floor and dunes of tan paper over deep blue midnight sky. Arrange crumpled towel and a book on Rousseau or sleeping problems or wildlife preservation.

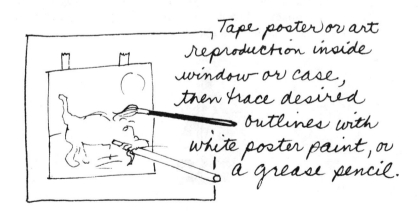

Tape poster or art reproduction inside window or case, then trace desired outlines with white poster paint, or a grease pencil.

Quartets

Floor display for books on related subjects, series of books (such as the *Raj Quartet*), books on music or biographies of composers.

Materials: 3, 4 or 5 music stands — borrowed from music department of
                school or community orchestra
             foam board, or sheet of plywood, for cut-out conductor, to
                be painted solid black, as a silhouette 5′ to 8′ high
             wood or concrete block dummy board stand
             foam board scraps or stiff cardboard for large music notes —
                8″ or 10″ high
             black poster paint
             3, 4, or 5 books for display (or photocopies of sheet music
                which can be borrowed from the library)

Technique: Cut out dummy board conductor on his stand — simplified is
                best. The baton can be added on, and taped to the dummy
                with black masking tape (use a black, artist's paintbrush han-
                dle, or a drumstick painted black). A heavy wood block with
                slot for dummy board, or two large bricks taped together, or
                an easel-back will hold the conductor up. Arrange music
                stands and hang notes above.

Books Really Perform

Poster or bulletin board, especially good if there's a big show in town. Always take advantage of well-publicized events going on in your town — if the circus is coming, do a circus-related display; if the baseball team just won a pennant, do a baseball-related display; if it's just rained for 10 straight weekends, do a sunny brighter-side display.

Materials: curtains: crepe paper or cloth
                  staple gun
                  deep blue poster board
                  light paper for cutting out books, or photocopy book
                      pages — perhaps on ballet or other performing art
                  Kraft paper for legs and arms and wood floorboards
                  paste or doubleface tape
                  felt pens

Technique: Staple narrow curtain border at top. Cut out bent and straight legs, and draw ballet shoes on with felt pen. Cut out tan floorboards and draw boards and woodgrain or leave plain. Position to get most action out of the dancers, paste down or use tape, then letter your headline.

Adaptation: Hang several books from ceiling of case or window. Attach pink or white tights, stuffed with tissue paper, and borrowed ballet shoes. Here's a good window for a small fan, which will cause the legs to move about.

BOOKS REALLY PERFORM

Tune-Up

Poster or bulletin board, with design useable for brochures and flyers, to advertise lunchtime concerts, music collection — records, sheet music, composer biographies, etc.

Materials: Kraft paper tan for hand
               rich brown Con-Tact™ paper or other glossy or semi-glossy
                   paper
               blue or black and white background poster board
               letters — these can be white if dark background is used

Technique: Cut out hand and cello or bass and draw simple details on.
               Use a ruler to draw cello strings (I didn't, and they need the
               taut straightness). Place up at top to form an arch, perhaps
               with dark paper at top and light paper below. Add lettering.

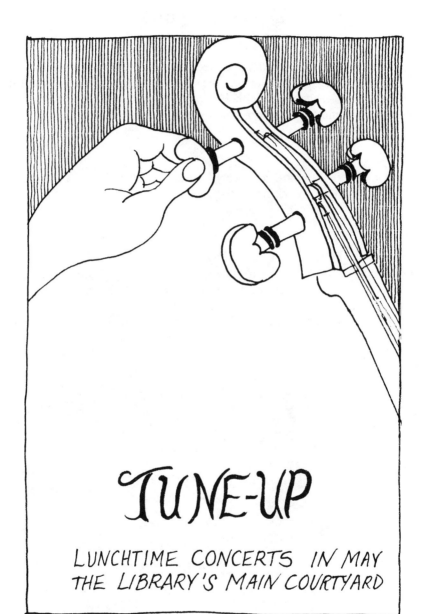

Dancing Figures

A mobile of lifesize figures to dance over browsing area or music books, etc. Based on a modern dance performance seen in 1985, where a huge mural of graffiti-cum-legit artist Keith Haring came alive, with huge dancing figures that joined in the choreography of the dancers.

Materials: foam board, probably 3 sheets 4 × 8
              heavy black felt pens
              nylon fishing line

Technique: Get volunteers to pose lying on the foam boards in agitated and exaggerated poses. Trace and cut, then draw the black outlines, especially for limbs that cross the torsos. Add simple features. String up from ceiling — air movement should keep them dancing lightly.

To do life-size figures, have adult or child pose lying on cardboard and trace around; omit details.

Night Blooming Jazz Men

Bulletin board or poster for celebrating jazz composers' birthdays, discographies, jazz books or records. Adaptable for 3-D display prop.

Materials: thick green rug yarn
green felt or construction paper
colored paper for faces
felt pen
poster board background
book jackets or facsimiles
craft glue

or

construction paper
florists' green-wrapped wire, or wire threaded through thick
   green rug yarn, or small tree branches
green spray paint
paper plates
big stapler

Technique: On poster board, pencil vine up side and along the top. Have
the craft glue and the yarn ready. Follow pencil line with glue,
and press yarn on it immediately. Cut flower faces from tan,
pink, yellow or brown paper; draw features with felt pen. Cut
petals from paper and glue or tape them to faces, then glue
faces (letting petals stick out) to board. Cut leaves from green
paper, or loop the yarn. Add book jackets, with doublesided
tape.

Adaptation: Make into case display with flower pots and small tree branches spray-painted green. Colored paper plates make perfect
faces; staple two together front to front. If you can do a case
display, add a few jazz instruments — a shiny sax and a drum,
which could serve as a book stand, would be good. Check
with the drum's owner about placing books on a tightened
drum head.

OR: VIBRATIONS , DAVID AMRAM
BIRD LIVES , ROSS RUSSELL
TO BE OR NOT TO BOP, DIZZY GILLESPIE

Gardening

Tree Products

Case display to attract curiosity seekers, and to show a range of products made from trees, on which the library has material. Rubber, coconut, lumber, books/paper, maple sugar, artists' turpentine.

Materials: several sawed off sections of a tree, small to large diameter
several colorful, plastic jug caps and a dishwashing detergent cap
"V" of wood to start the headline "W"
felt pen – brown or black
household or carpenters' glue

Technique: Place wood sections with caps in place. Add blocks or cards on various subjects. Or make paper labels – "Turpentine" "Maple Sugar" – to put on wood sections. Or do one on maple sugar alone, with sugaring bucket, plate, cardboard pancakes with polyurethane syrup, maple sugar mold, maple tap, and a section of wood made up with label and cap.

Cabbages and Kings

Poster for vegetarian cookbooks, or vegetable cookery and gardening in general.

Materials: white poster board
black and red felt markers
green construction papers in two shades
glue

Technique: Sketch out your king holding his cabbage stalk scepter on a big piece of newsprint, even newspaper. Cut out to use to trace on poster board. If the poster is to be 36" high, the king and cabbage should be about 15" high. Trace, then draw in details like beard, crown, eyes and ermine spots. Cut cabbage leaves from green paper and affix, or color leaves green. Draw the pot and spoon with red marker, and whatever lettering you wish.

Adaptation: If you have a male manikin, dress like king and put real cabbage in his hands. Station near cookbooks. Sign: "Eat Royally."

The Vegetarian World

Poster for film entitled "The Vegetarian World," or for display of vegetarian books.

Materials: colored paper large enough to create poster. Orange paper for carrot can be smaller sheets, with sections joined. Green and tan paper for director's chair; black patent paper for sunglasses (you may find a shoe box or shopping bag of shiny black paper); green paper for leaves
white or pale green poster board
paste or doublesided tape
felt-tip pen

Technique: Cut out carrot and canvas parts of director's chair (the legs can be cut out or you can draw on). Cut out sunglasses and scraggly-fuzzy leaves (look at real carrot leaves for reference). Paste or tape into place on posterboard. Letter after lightly penciling placement.

Adaptation: Set up a real director's chair in a case or window, create a carrot from two or three sheets of orange poster board (or a foam board, painted orange), use real sunglasses and yarn or plastic ferns for leaves. You may have to tape carrot into chair.

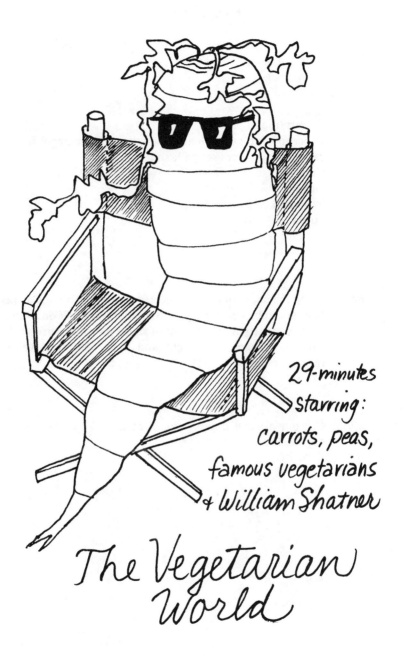

29-minutes
starring:
carrots, peas,
famous vegetarians
& William Shatner

The Vegetarian
World

Pet Plants

Display case for plant lovers.

Materials: flowerpot and plant
paper to wrap pot with and enough matching paper for legs
cat/dog toys — mouse, ball, squeak toy
show
glove
leash and collar
books
background and floor paper

Technique: Wrap the pot with paper — spotted is nice and obviously pet-like, and tape cut out legs. Put collar and leash on. Attach glove upper right, almost out of sight; put shoe, with stuffed stocking perhaps, at far right, and attach leash to glove. Arrange toys and book(s).

Adaptation: Cut out a small dummy board of a barking plant with a doglike head.

Cut out paper legs to tape with double-side cellophane tape to sides of flowerpot.

BARK BARK

Patron Participation

Clubs, Contests, Etc.

Garden Fund

Watch Us Grow! (or Help Us Grow!)

Spring or summer if you use a growing sunflower or daisy; anytime for a growing giant or Jack and the Bookstalk. Marks level of contributions.

Materials: string or colored yarn, braided green/brown yarn for stalk, green felt leaves, yellow felt and gold carpet sample flower, watering can, bricks, 2 pulleys and a pair of hooks or nails, paper on which to draw growth chart

Technique: Affix pulleys to ceiling, near a wall, or further out, in which case the growth chart will have to be noted nearby. Braid yarn or green string for stem, attach cut-out leaves, make flower of carpet sample center with felt petals. Attach one end of stem to floor. String the pulleys, and wrap the 2 hooks or nails with the end, like a window shade cord. Set watering can on wall of bricks — weight it substantially with bricks, and take out money frequently. Mark the various levels, and amounts. When levels reached, make flower grow.

Adaptations: Create a giant book/bean stalk for children's room. Have it grow each day or week — the last week of a period, affix a Jack and a Giant — Jack at the base, Giant at the top. Or make a very long paper building out of sheets of red or gray paper, taped together end to end. Each time the **Building Fund** grows, another section or two of the bricks rise up from the folded pile at the floor. For a **Computer Fund**, use computer paper, which will unfold magnificently from a compact pile.

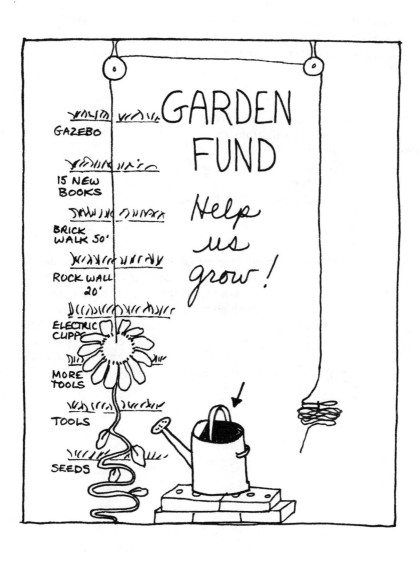

Halley's Comet Club Pins

Pins to award to club members — membership being those youngsters or people interested in forming a comet watching group, or who have read all they can about the comet's history and would like to discuss it.

Materials: cardboard discs or buttons
               yellow paper (buttons should be yellow)
               yellow yarn
               safety pins
               strong tape
               permanent marker for lettering

Technique: Cardboard disc can be covered with bright yellow paper on the front, and have 3 loops of yarn, in 3 different lengths, taped to back, then a safety pin taped on. The button can have loops of yarn put through the holes, tied in back, and a safety pin put through the knot. Letter fronts with markers. You could also buy a pinback button machine, create artwork that is photocopied and put under the plastic that encapsulates it for the button. (See materials list at end.)

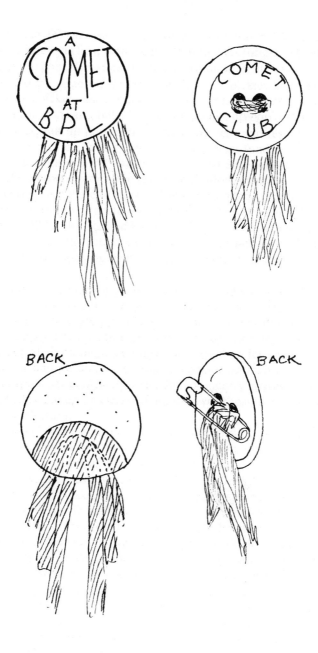

Halley's Comet

Case display, bookmark and folder for the coming of Halley's Comet.

Materials: large piece of dark blue paper to fit front of case or window
or, acrylic paint, dark blue, which can be easily removed
wide paint brush
aluminum foil
yellow & white acrylic paint
ladder — even a step ladder
sign
book

Technique: Cut dark blue paper (see if you can get leftover piece of
photographer's no-seam paper after a shoot — they usually
throw out) to fit front glass. Glue on aluminum foil stars, or
cut out stars. Cut out center hole, and, using a fairly dry
brush, paint the comet's tail in yellow and white streaks. Tape
into window. Arrange ladder, poster and book(s). The idea is
to keep the viewing hole reasonably small. Print bookmark
and flyer on blue paper with white, or print white paper with
blue — lettering and sky.

Event: Have a "Twice in a Lifetime" program with those citizens who
recall the 1910 passing of comet.

Time Capsule

A 3-D object and the accompanying form, for the public to participate in the creation of a real or imaginary time capsule.

Materials: very large round box — such as a Quaker Oats box
paper for label, including clock face
silver stick-on stars
photocopied fill-in forms

Technique: Cover box being careful not to seal up lid. Make clock face, with years — 1985, 1990, 1995, 2000, etc. — instead of numbers. Cut slot in bottom, for that will be the top. Type a fill-in form, lay out so that 4 will fit on one 8 ½ × 11 sheet, photocopy on colored paper. Limit the time alotted for contributing suggestions to a month or so so that people don't lose interest and forget. Tabulate the results and type up to hand out, along with booklist of futurist books, or books with time travel or time capsules in them.

WHAT WOULD YOU PUT IN A **TIME CAPSULE?**

TIME CAPSULE FOR OURTOWN

NAME _____ ADDRESS _____

CITY _____ ZIP _____ PHONE _____

FOUR THINGS I'D ENCLOSE: (1) _____

(2) _____ (3) _____ (4) _____

I COULD SUPPLY ( ) ( ) ( ) ( ) FOR A REAL CAPSULE.

WHEN IT SHOULD BE OPENED _____ COMMENTS (OVER)

People Reading Photo Contest

Poster with attached forms for entering a contest that should make people look out for, and perhaps thereby encourage, readers.

Materials: black poster board
               bright yellow construction paper
               transparent tape
               light gray construction paper
               paste
               black felt pen
               photocopied forms
               heavy duty stapler

Technique: Cut out large yellow film canister. Join several sheets of gray paper in a sort of snaky pattern and sketch the film edge then cut. Paste to poster board. Letter, with marker or with some plastic lettering. Staple on photocopied form.

Adaptation: Use white 8 ½ × 11 paper and draw can and film in black, with some heavy lettering such as *Photo Contest*. Then photocopy on "goldenrod" offset paper — enough posters to go up all over town.

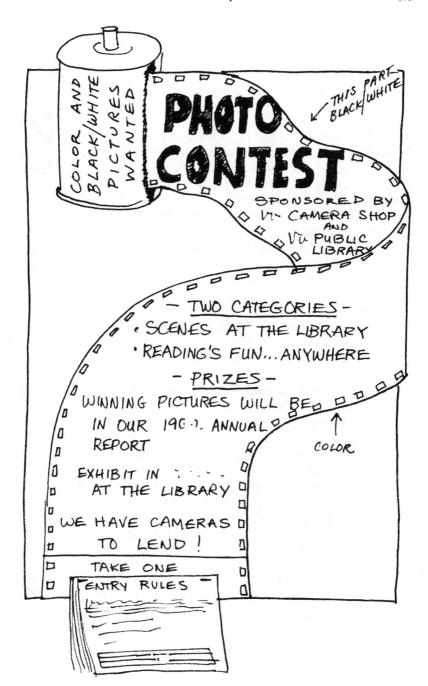

Library Pastry

This is a two-forked idea: a recipe contest first, then a fundraiser recipe booklet that you can sell.

Using the term "pastry" fairly loosely, advertise widely for original or adapted recipes for cookies, cakes, dessert quick breads, pies, dumplings, tarts, turnovers, sweetrolls, raisin or popcorn balls. Emphasize that recipes must, if adapted, credit the source to avoid copyright trouble. (Also, so that you can check the recipes against citations.) Put notices up in groceries, health food shops, in the library's cookbook section. Think of special outreachings—to cooks and waitresses in local restaurants; employees at local plants; bridge clubs; retirement homes.

Encourage people to pun their hearts out with names and ingredients. Use your own judgment about testing recipes. It may be possible for people to bring their pastries to the library for sampling. Remember this is fun, not Cordon Bleu.

Children can be included with a division of their own. If children are solicited *first*, great publicity pictures can be made of them cooking up their recipes, or decorating the results.

An easy cookbook format, used often for fundraiser cookbooks, comprises offset pages, usually half an 8½" × 11" sheet, one recipe per page. Someone might do line drawings for decoration. Stiff cardboard covers can be printed with a bold design, or decorated (in another children's project) with rubber stamps. The left side of each sheet gets two punched holes, and the "binding" is two snap rings. A 50-page book (about ¼" thick) will require ½" or ¾" rings.

Public libraries can work with local schools, perhaps calling on the Home Ec. classes to test recipes, for full credit in the book. Sharing means sharing profits and costs. School libraries may stay within the school—getting recipes from students, teachers staff and parents—or they may want to solicit recipes from local shopkeepers, retired people, the fire department, etc.

A "Library Pasta" contest might be preferred—with recipes for homemade spaghetti, macaroni or noodles, plus the sauces.

"Orange Bright" Cake

"Orange bright, like golden lamps in a green night."—Andrew Marvell

1 orange peel, grated
1 orange peel, trimmed of white and minced
water to cover
½ cup brown sugar
½ cup butter (1 stick)
2 eggs
½ cup thawed orange juice concentrate
1 cup milk
2¼ cups all-purpose flour
3 teaspoons baking powder
1 teaspoon salt
¼ cup chopped pecans/walnuts

Cooke the grated and minced orange *Peele* in a small saucepan, in just enough water to cover, for five minutes. *Cool*idge to room temperature. (Now preheat oven to 350° F.) Cream the butter and *Browne* sugar in a large mixing bowl, and mix in the orange peel. Beating like the *Dickens*, mix in the eggs, one at a time. Add orange juice concentrate and milk, and stir. Put half the flour in a large sifter, then salt and baking powder, then the remaining flour. Sift one third of the dry ingredients into the liquid mixture, stirring thoroughly. Add another third and stir; put the final third in with the nuts and beat 35 *Hardy* strokes — fewer if you want it more like bread. Turn into a greased and flour-dusted loaf pan, approximately 8½" × 4½" × 2½" deep. Bake about 50 minutes until *Dunne*. Turn out on a *Rack*ham, cool thoroughly before wrapping. Wait a *Day* to serve and it'll slice better. You'll *Marvell* at the taste, and so will other *Foulke*!

Developing Character

Marketing directors have discovered how lucrative characters are. Look through some general interest magazines of the 1940s and see the Dutch Cleanser girl, the Dutch Boy who sold paint, the little girl on the salt box, the Bon Ami chick who "hasn't scratched yet," even Betty Crocker herself — all characters used in advertising to enlist consumer loyalty to a brand by building a personal bond akin to friendship.

Characters are also used to sell themselves; *they* are the product. From the wimpy pink Strawberry Shortcake to the voracious Pac-Man, there is something to appeal to every consumer. They identify the persona of each character, as it can be observed in action on TV, resting on posters and magazine ads, or manifested in the flesh in dolls and toys and other 3-D goods. The persona is either attractive or repellent to an individual. The attraction each person may feel to one or more characters — out of all the thousands — is as inexplicable as that felt about real people, although more simplistic. It is probably often akin to the attraction most people feel towards the young of all species. In fact, a psychological study of Mickey Mouse's worldwide appeal concluded that Mickey's large head (proportioned to his body like the head of any baby, human or animal), his large eyes and his rounded shape accounted for most of it.

One approach to getting people to think of the library, and librarians, as a primary source for answers to personal problems, for information helpful to everyday life, and for culture to improve the quality of life, might be to create a character. This character would express some desirable personal traits, and would incorporate libraric and local symbols, totems, features, tags or traits. If the library were in Minnesota, for example, where the loon and the mosquito vie for position as "state bird," perhaps something could be taken from one or both. *Loony* is pejorative, but it could be played on, even turned around: with the help of the library, not loony any more. If the library were in Maine, a character might be found in a sea captain, a stowaway, a fishing trawler, a sea gull or a school of fish. If the library were in Hershey, Pennsylvania, where *everything* is chocolate, one more chocolateness is possible.

The ideal character is versatile and can be made of simple materials and in different sizes and for different display uses. A Denver librarian at the 1982 July A.L.A. Conference asked about creating interest in their children's and school departments. Knowing that Denver is the "Mile High City," I suggested a very tall, long-legged bird marionette, called "Mile High Bird." With flexible gangly legs and weighted feet, M.H.B. could be suspended from the ceiling over the children's room, or made to sit on top of a shelf, or manipulated so its feet could be planted on various tables, desks or shelves. Spin-offs — in the form of bookmarks or coloring pages or other cheap giveaways — could range from "Inch High Bird" (for the fledgling reader) to "Foot High Bird" to "Yard Bird," and be awarded following completion of reading programs. Diplomas, another form of incentive, could be stamped with a picture of the appropriate bird level and its name. Rubber stamps can be made photographically from drawings — keep the lines simple and comparatively thick. "Mile High Bird" could be used on posters, in case or window displays, even as a goodwill visitor to schools, children's hospital wards, local stores' toy departments, at Audubon Society filmings, etc. Think as broadly as you like — postcards, hand puppet contests, costume parties for readers.

If you create a character and it becomes widely known and identified strongly with your library, or a department or service in your library, you will be using one of the most successful marketing strategies for promoting products and services. The possibilities are endless.

See Materials Appendix under "Animated Displays."

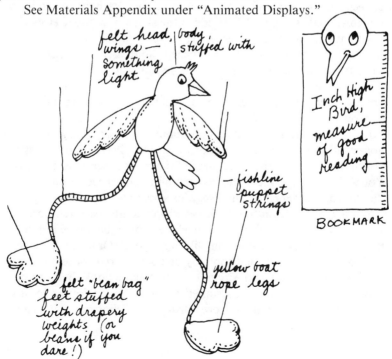

felt head, body,
wings — stuffed with
something
light

— fishline
puppet
strings

Inch High
Bird,
measure
of good
reading

BOOKMARK

felt "bean bag"
feet stuffed
with drapery
weights (or
beans if you
dare!)

yellow boat
rope legs

A Library Boutique

Most art museums have some kind of gift shop. Often it's the most frequented footage in the building, even bringing people in off the street who have no intention of going around the galleries to look at art. On the other hand, relatively few libraries have gift shops, although it's a natural project for a Friends of the Library group, or other volunteer organization.

Patrons of the grand New York Public Library are delighted that the shop of wonders is again open. Included in the stock are beautifully printed notecards with art taken from the library's print collection; new postcards of the library plus other literary subjects; old postcards of New York; various puzzles and games; book bags and other items carrying the lion image; plus notepads and pens and pencils.

You and your library have as much access to suitable items as NYPL. Many things may originate in your library itself (stationery items based on the collection, for example) or from your locality. Perhaps a craft person in your town makes walnut bookends in the shape of a book. How about that, with an arranged percentage? Art students in high school or college might create one or a series of silkscreened, limited-edition posters.

The following suggestions ought to be followed:

- Write up a very brief and general proposal for submission to the library's trustees and legal department.
- Request information from tax offices about how your library (public and nonprofit) must deal with bookkeeping, tax collection and reporting.
- Broach the subject with your Library Friends or other volunteer group. You will need a manager (who may double as bookkeeper) who oversees the shop and orders merchandise, plus assistants who can wait on people, bring things from the stockroom, operate the cash register.
- Figure out the space you'll need, and where it might be carved out. Something in the area of the browsing library is good. Or if you have an exhibition room or hall, that too may be good shared space.
- Decide if you can make do with a few tables and a book shelf or two, at least at first. Card racks can sometimes be obtained from a local stationery shop or department store during remodeling but you'd have to

be lucky to be there at the right time. Racks or card shelves for the wall are an easy carpentry job, to be modeled after those in a card shop.
- Decide what kind of merchandise you want to offer and what specific lines of the many manufacturers are best for you. You can do a lot of preliminary investigation in card shops. Armed with a list of manufacturers, you can use various directories in your own reference department to contact manufacturers' sales offices. They can refer you to local or traveling reps.
- Think about creating something special for the library — enthusiasm for tee-shirts has not waned and they are still popular "collector items." Bookbags, buttons, posters, greeting cards (especially for Christmas or birthdays) — all are good bets.
- Start small, because you'll be learning as you go, but have enough variety so that one visit won't exhaust all the buyer's needs. Keep adding (and subtracting) items.
- Advertise within the library itself. And, if it's legal for you to do so, advertise around town. If you stock items that really fit the library, you won't be treading on the toes of local stationers or card and gift shops.

Things to Consider Selling

What's the library all about? All libraries, and yours in particular. Certainly a pen and paper are very basic — both in creating the books you now treasure, and in doing research from them. Also the communication of ideas ... in film, pictures, sounds and words.

Books — (NYPL stocks Dover, some children's books, some writing/reading references and stylebooks). Consider pocket-size foreign language dictionaries, Strunk & White on style, film history, writers' guides, etc. There are a number of publishers of books — scholarly and reference — for libraries, books with no bookstore outlet. Investigate some of these: often the public would be interested if they knew about such books.

Cards & Stationery — some manufacturers offer notecards with reproductions of everything from Japanese scrolls to Delft tiles.

Notepads — yellow lined pads, 8½ × 11 or legal size; simple 5 × 7 white paper pads.

Ballpoint Pens & Pencils — these are, like the notepads, convenience items for library patrons, rather than gift items.

Erasers — you could offer amusingly-shaped erasers, or utilitarian art gum and rubber erasers.

Pocket-Size Pencil Sharpeners

Postcards — you would probably be amazed at how inexpensive it is to have postcards made. Printed in colored ink on fairly substantial paper, in quantities of 5,000–7,500 you can have cards printed for under $500. Reproduce a wonderful line-cut from an old book (do investigate copyright), or a woodcut in the print collection, or an original work of art. Or reproduce a bookish or filmic image taken from one of the many "pick-up" art books, such as those published by Dover.

Old Postcards — there may be an active deltiology club in your locale, and it's quite possible they'll have a 10¢ box. *You* can sell them for a quarter.

Posters — art posters, humorous posters, film or movie posters, perhaps even a few that promote libraries. Have you seen the marvelous Mickey Mouse READ poster offered by the American Library Association's Public Information office?

Blank Books — these come in a wide variety of covers and sizes, many of them quite decorative. Crown and Quillmark are two big manufacturers. Semiblank hardcover books, illustrated with turn-of-the-century art, are offered by Tree Communications. Paper-cover books with theme illustrations are offered by Running Press Artists' sketchbooks, particularly the hardbound ones, are another sort of blank book.

Bookends — decorative and utilitarian.

Wooden Type Faces — sell the individual letters. These are sometimes available at a flea market or when a printer goes out of business.

Radio Spots

Most libraries, because they are nonprofit, will make use of the Federal Communications Commission's requirement that radio stations broadcast — free of charge — announcements concerning programs, activities, or services of such nonprofit organizations, instead of buying commercial time.

PSAs (Public Service Announcements), which are sometimes referred to as PSBs (or Bulletins), are either local or national; we are concerned here only with local ones. They can be quite general and meant to give an impressionistic picture of what the library has to offer, or they can be written to announce a particular event or service — usually one of limited duration or one that is to occur on a specific date. Some PSAs are in the form of scripts, to be read live by the announcer, or they can be taped by the library, and offered to the stations in tape form, with an accompanying script.

The best and fullest explanation of preparing PSAs that I have read is in David R. Yale's *The Publicity Handbook*. Almost as useful, with some facts from another point of view, is David Tedone's *Practical Publicity!* (Both books are in the Bibliography.)

According to David Yale, and others, PSAs range in length from 10 to 60 seconds, and because of demand for air time, shorter ones are more likely to be read and aired frequently. Don't plunge into writing or taping PSAs without consulting program directors or public relations directors of each radio station that you hope will broadcast your message. They may lend you technical assistance or provide recording time; at the very least they'll give you guidelines as to content, or structure, and length. They may tell you right away that they want only 10-second PSAs, or only 30 second ones that can be cut (possibly by the station).

Generally speaking, you get about 20 to 25 words for 10 seconds, and anyone who has written classified ads knows how tightly written and successful such a short message can be. David Yale suggests that you should "consider using two voices," because the PSA will sound less "monotonous" — and, more importantly — "less of a pause between sentences" will be required. Two voices, like music or sound effects, add a touch of drama too. But these things can only be written for a PSA that is taped for broadcast.

The examples that follow are meant only to suggest a range of possibilities, and they use a variety of techniques or inspirations: borrowing or adapting quotes of famous writers; borrowing key—even cliché—phrases from advertising lingo; using rhyme.

(1) *(Whispered)*: You don't have to whisper at the library.
    (Normal voice): The books all speak for themselves ... so can you. Listen at the Library; 10 to 6 all week. *(10 seconds.)*

(2) New! Improved! Paperbacks of best sellers published just this year. No waiting ... we've got hundreds! The downtown library, open late on Thursdays. *(10 seconds.)*

(3) For a diet high in moral fiber, the library has a variety of new and old books on ethics, religion and philosophy. The public library. It helps you grow. *(10 seconds.)*

(4) Get into a book that fits! All styles and lengths. The library suits all the best-read people in * * *. *(8 seconds.)*

(5) Find out what 100 famous people have to say about life, love, taxes, war, peace, art, and the future. They're all in one room: the Biography section at the library. Today and every weekday. *(12 seconds.)*

(6) *(First voice)*: Some books are to be tasted *(smack lips)*, others to be swallowed, and some few to be chewed and digested.
    (Second voice): Francis Bacon, may I have another helping?
    (First voice): Sure! At the library, we've got a very appetizing menu. *(14 seconds.)*

(7) Down ... and out of books? The * * * Library has a new bedside manner: the Hospital Lending Program. To find out more, call 333-5555. That's 333-5555. *(10 seconds.)*

(8) *(Sounds of typing, hammering, electronic bells.)* Trained counselors at the public library's Job Center will help you in your search for new skills. 10 to 2 every weekday, at 555 Main Street. *(hammering, typing, bells.)* The * * * Library. We're not as quiet as we used to be! *(About 20 seconds.)*

(9) Abe Lincoln said "The things I want to know are in books," and Will Rogers said "All I know is just what I read in the papers." The things *you* want to know are probably in the library. If not in a book or paper, we'll get out something else. The * * * Library. *(About 20 seconds.)*

(10) Our candles burn on both floors,/ They will not last the night./ At nine p.m. we lock our doors.../ Until the morning light. *(Pause.)* For authentic Edna St. Vincent Millay poems, and more, see you at the library, 9 to 9, rain or shine. *(16 seconds.)*

(11) A friend to everybody is a friend to nobody. That's why the library has all kinds of books, records, tapes and magazines ... so you can choose your own friends. *(10 seconds.)*

(12) Neither a borrower nor a lender be,/ Except at the public li-brar-y! *(5 seconds.)*

(13) *(Rather like the old Howdy Doody "Mickey Mouse" chant)*: V-A-R-I-E-T-Y/ L-I-B-R-A-R-Y/ We have got va-ri-e-ty,/ At the public li-brar-y! *(10 seconds.)*

(14) *(Rather like a rap)*: Don't keep goin' on and on/ Blabbin' blah-blah all night long./ Throw aside your hesitation,/ Trade it in for cogitation./ We've got books won't make you yawn,/ Though you read from dusk to dawn./ Grandmaster Brain ... at the public library. *(13 seconds.)*

(15) Up with the birds now that spring is here? The * * * library has early-bird bookworm hours every Tuesday this summer. Check it out ... starting at 7 a.m.! *(10 seconds.)*

User Friendly Quotes
for Posters, Brochures, Publicity

His cogitative faculties immersed
In cogibundity of cogitation.
— *Henry Carey (c.1693–1743)*.

> A good book is the best of friends,
> the same today and for ever.
> — *Martin Tupper (1810–1889)*.

The medicine chest of the soul.
— *Ancient Greek inscription on a library*.

> In knowledge unseen, as in hidden treasure,
> there is no utility.   — *Old saying*.

[*For a display of biographies*]: The privilege that is waiting in the great
biographies [is] to know people whom to know living would have been
worth a king's ransom, but could not have been bought at any price, to
read their letters, to see their mistakes, to know their love affairs, to
watch them deal with their handicaps, work out their philosophies of
life, meet their sorrows, face their advancing age, and fall on death, one
wonders why people who want nothing but entertainment read the
trivial trash that the presses grind out while such a rich feast of human
interest is awaiting them.
— *Harry Emerson Fosdick, "Blessed Be Biography,"*
Ladies' Home Journal, 1924.

[*For children's reading program, or book selection*]: I was left to myself
to find my own provender in the library. If you do that with a child, he
will always take the nourishment that is suitable to him, just as when
you look over a meadow over which cattle are grazed you will find certain grasses are taken and certain are rejected. You may depend on it

that the cow knows what is suitable to her own health. It is the same with the child. You may leave the child with perfect safety in any library you like, and if that child has a natural turn for books he will take the right sustenance and thrive on it.
—*Stanley Baldwin, speech at the English Association, 1927.*

Write me a verse, my old machine —
    I lack for an inspiration;
The skies are blue and the trees are green,
    And I long for a long vacation.
—*Edwin Meade Robinson* (with this quote, you might set up a typewriter, and ask patrons to type in couplets on some subject chosen as the Subject of the Week).

    I love vast libraries; yet there is doubt
    If one be better with them or without, —
    Unless he use them wisely, and, indeed,
    Knows the high art of what and how to
    read.
    —*J.G. Saxe, "The Library."*

No place affords a more striking conviction of the vanity of human hopes, than a public library.
—*Samuel Johnson, "The Rambler," March 23, 1751.*

A professor can never better distinguish himself in his work than by encouraging a clever pupil, for the true discoverers are among them, as comets amongst the stars.   —*Carl Linnaeus.*

   "Dream of a Spelling Bee"
Menageries where sluth hounds caracole,
Where jaguar phalanx and phlegmatic gnu
Fright ptarmigan and kestrels cheek by jowl
With peewit and precocious cockatoo.

Gaunt seneschals, in crotchety cockades,
With seine net trawl for porpoise in lagoons;
While scullions gauge erratic escapades
Of madrepores in water-logged galleons.

Flamboyant triptychs groined with gherkins green,
In reckless fracas with coquettish bream,
Ecstatic gargoyles, with grotesque chagrin,
Garnish the gruesome nightmare of my dream.
—*Quoted in "Record of the Year," March 7, 1876.
Originally from Punch."*

Books are a part of man's prerogative,
In formal ink their thought and voices hold,
That we to them our solitude may give,
And make time present travel that of old.
Our life, fame pierceth longer at the end,
And books it farther backward doth extend.
— *Sir Thomas Overbury.*

God has made the intellectual world harmonious and beautiful without us; but it will never come into our heads all at once; we must bring it home piece-meal, and there set it up by our own industry, or else we shall have nothing but darkness and a chaos within, whatever order and light there be in things without us.
— *John Locke, "An Essay Concerning Human Understanding," 1690.*

Man is not the only animal that talks. Monkeys chatter and signal to each other, crows caw, bees direct each other to new sources of food by intricate dances. But man is the only animal who can talk from one century or millennium to another. And we do it through books and libraries.
— *Robert D. Franklin, in the "Toledo Public Library Annual Report," 1959.*

Invest in your library today: put in some money and take out some books.
— *Grace McFarland.*

Library Newsletters

In this age, many groups of professionals or hobbyists adopt this relatively inexpensive way to disseminate information, which may or may not — strictly speaking — be "news." A newsletter that fosters a sense of community among all staffers, or among members of a Friends group, is done with reports of past and future events, and newsy items about members and the library or organization. The intent can be to further a cause or course of action, increase attendance, or merely entertain.

At its simplest, a newsletter records facts and figures, with a leavening of anecdotes. Another may run similar items but written to entice new library users by showing off a little. A third type may be a vehicle for expressing visions, opinions, or innovations, and the readership is likely to be professionals, politicians or fundraising sources who matter to the newsletter's author.

Outline the sorts of subjects that will best get your communication job done. Draw on aspects of your library that are the newest, most successful, or most underutilized. Make a list: *strong in current fiction, *upholstered chairs with armrests, *expanded bookmobile routes, *fulltime job counseling, *photo contest, *new main entrance ramp, *10 borrowable VCRs, *opening of picnic grounds for lunchtime reading. Such subjects are also suitable for press releases to local media.

Format & Size: This includes general appearance, presentation, formality, and the number of pages. Typewriters with daisy wheels or print balls or word processing computers hooked to printers with a choice of faces offer great flexibility, and photostatic enlargements add to the range of type sizes. The most expensive option is typesetting. Will you use one or both sides of an 8½ × 11 sheet; one or both sides of an 8½ × 14 sheet; two such sheets stapled together for two or four pages; or an 11 × 17 sheet printed both sides, folded to make four pages? Will you use inexpensive paper, perhaps different colors each issue?

Reproduction: Is the newsletter to be photocopied, perhaps on a library machine? Or is offset printing better because hundreds will be needed?

Distribution Method: Is the newsletter only for staff, or Friends meetings, or to be handed out in places around the city, or mailed out? The answers help determine the size and weight of paper used, and how and if it is folded. Envelopes add expense, weight and time spent.

It is easy, and psychologically upbeat, to increase the size or complicate the format and presentation. You might start with a one-page letter with one clip-book illustration and a nice masthead or logo, and later add pages and more pictures or even photos, or go from typewritten to typeset copy, or go from being "occasional" to monthly. Don't be afraid to start small!

One person must be in charge, but several people can do the work. The newsletter is easiest if very informal, with very short news clips that present names, dates and locations in a standard format. These items may be contributed by staffers on a regular basis, and should include upcoming events far enough in advance that they will still be in the future when the letter comes out. A good clip art book, or a staff artist, can contribute simple little line illustrations that add eye appeal. Every issue may have sections such as *Personal Notes, Art & Antiques News, Suggestion Box Selections, Scary New Mysteries*, etc.

Cranking One Out

Say one person is going to do a single sheet 8½ × 11, printed both sides, to be offset and mailed without an envelope, to enough people to warrant getting a bulk mail permit which, in 1985, costs $50 and covers mail sent to 200 + addresses. Here's how:

1. Send a note to each department (clerical, maintenance and professional) requesting news items to be routed to you in a particular format, say printed or typed on a 3 × 5 p-slip. Discourage spur-of-the-moment, intercom tidbit calls.

2. Assemble all gathered items and sort by subject or section. If you are lucky, you'll have a lot of items, only some of which must be used right away. Sort again, with two issues in mind.

3. Write a list of items in brief outline, each under its appropriate section headline. Is the list balanced and interesting?

4. Jot down notes about illustrations — what you have in mind, or what is suggested by a particular item.

5. Edit items to conform to a simple style, and type all of them, straight across the paper, single-spaced. Leave 1½″ margins left, bottom, and right, and leave 3″ to 4″ at the top for the masthead. You need about 44 single-spaced lines, including headline lines, for the first page, and about 39 lines for the second page.

If you have too little, select another item; or copy a quote that's worth sharing, with its full credit. Or fill in with pictures. Type an item "short," that is, only ¾ of the width of the page, and put a picture in the last ¼ of space. Or, if you have a picture with irregular outlines, trace around it on a clean piece of paper and retype.

6. Create a masthead from library stationery, or clip art, or draw something that stands for your library and communication issuing from it. Shown here is the masthead for the highly regarded *Tee-Pee*, done for the TPL (Toledo Public Library) for many years by its director, Robert D. Franklin. Visual puns enliven the newsletter. The masthead may include the

full name and address of the library and or the sponsoring organization; some indication of the proposed frequency; a volume number and issue number; and perhaps the name of the person doing it, although this may also go at the end, as a sign-off.

7. Roll fresh paper in typewriter, and align edges perfectly. Leave room for masthead, and start typing the items just as you worked them out, single-spaced.

8. Use another piece of paper for the second side, and leave the bottom third blank. This is for addressing. (See top of page 196.)

9. Use a glue stick to attach line drawings in place. To use photographs, you must have a "screen" photostat made, that will break the full tones of a color or black and white photo into what are called *half tones*, with dots or lines. These photostats are sometimes called Veloxes. At the same time, you can have the photograph *sized* — enlarged or made smaller — so it fits perfectly into the space allowed. Attach the masthead design, or a photostat of it, to the top of the first page. In the bottom third of the second page, put the library's return address at upper left.

10. Take the offset printer your two camera-ready sheets, called *mechanicals*. Select paper — probably 20# offset, white or any color. Leftover paper, for smallish runs of 200–500, may be available at bargain prices. Ask about accurate count policy. Some printers are under or over by 10%; others make it policy to always overrun. For the best price, an out-of-town printer may be the answer for you, as it is for me.

11. Instruct the printer about folding the sheets in thirds, and make sure the bottom third, where the address will be, is "out."

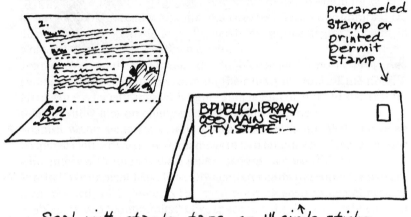

Seal with staple, tape or 1" circle sticker or, if fold is tight, no seal .

12. When you get the finished newsletters, have an addressing party. Self-adhesive labels are quickest and easiest, and special types are made for copiers—one for normal, one for high-temp copiers. You type a master sheet of addresses, and photocopy the labels as many times as necessary. Or feed a roll of gummed labels, which must be moistened, into the typewriter. This is much cheaper, but much more time-consuming, and it is hard to get a master list copy, and impossible to use a copier to duplicate. For special newsletter issues, say for parties or fundraisers, you may want to handwrite addresses.

13. If you have more than 200 pieces to mail, investigate bulk mailing. You can arrange to print a permit "stamp" directly on the newsletter, or you can buy precanceled stamps with your permit and affix them as you would a regular stamp.

14. As soon as the newsletters are in the mail, keep your momentum up by doing preliminary work on the next issue! Consider adding a *Letters* column, if you expect reader mail. Or solicit mail by requesting *Tricky Questions*, or requests for *Odd Facts*. Keep a file of ideas, pictures and suggestions.

Opposite: You can put the masthead in different places; you can have one, two or three column widths; you can place pictures in a variety of ways.

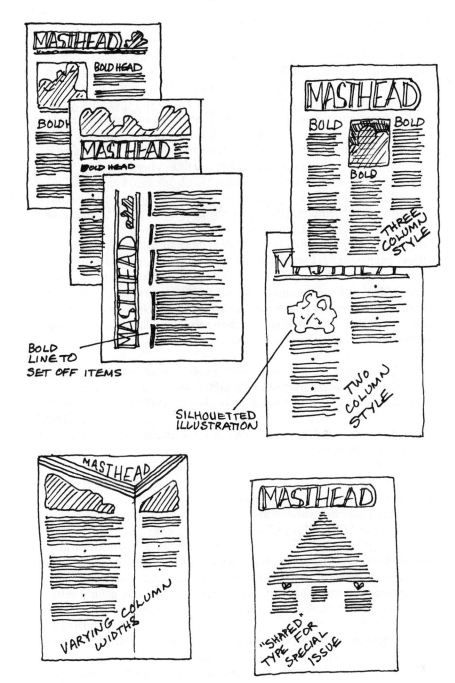

BOLD
LINE TO
SET OFF ITEMS

SILHOUETTED
ILLUSTRATION

THREE
COLUMN
STYLE

TWO
COLUMN
STYLE

VARYING COLUMN
WIDTHS

"SHAPED"
TYPE FOR
SPECIAL
ISSUE

Briefly Outlined Ideas:
Displays, Bulletin Boards,
Events & Public Relations
You Take Them from Here

The first 29 entries in this section are primarily display or bulletin board ideas. Many have PR potential, and many are related to special events. The remaining 29 entries are primarily publicity events, or public relations ideas. Many of them have attendant displays suggested. You can use some of the techniques and concepts for designs, lettering, and the use of made or found objects in the illustrated section of this book to develop the following outlines to suit your needs.

Keep a clip file in which you put newspaper and magazine reports of displays that have caught the public eye as well as publicity events and public relations campaigns. Often a single line in an article will lead you to a perfect solution to a problem the library has. Be sure to mark and annotate any clippings for this file — memory is fleeting, and a particular apt synaptic connection may occur but once. Don't be left with the bewildered question, "Why did I clip this?"

Displays and Bulletin Boards

Didja Know? Do a series of "Didja Know" bulletin boards. For example, "Didja know that this library owns a _____, and you can borrow it?" "Didja know that this library runs a _____ program for the elderly?" "Didja know that Librarian M.M. Booker can tell you just about anything about _____?" Or make questions more specific: "Didja know that there are 14 kinds of sparrows in our neighborhood?" Use to introduce specific subject areas in the collection, special books or encyclopedias, new or sometimes hidden-away staffers, your reference service. Business questions can be used in a flyer sent out to business people; nursery-school-age puppet show facilities sent out to daycare centers and churches; etc. Put up on freestanding standards which can be placed anywhere in the library. This article of furniture is very versatile.

That's Astonishing! Invite readers to fill out p-slips with the most astounding or fascinating thing — in one or two sentences, with source — they learned in the library that visit or week. Use a standard or wall bulletin board area, with question mark and exclamation point anthropomorphized with expressions of astonishment. Can be used for very unusual photographs found in newspapers from other areas or countries that most readers may have never seen.

Local Bird Census. Create a large chart, perhaps on a 4 × 8 foam board, with at least 200–300 birds listed down the left side, all the space to the right divided up into little squares for patrons to put a small check after the name of each bird they have seen in your locality or state. There may be so many checks after "robin" or "English sparrow" that you'll run out of space; consider two lines for checkmarks, or limit time frame of chart. Invite local birdwatchers or bird census takers to be on hand for a seminar, or demonstration of using binoculars, or how to build a blind, how to photograph wild birds, how to make a birdhouse. Sponsor a birdhouse contest — don't limit to children and adolescents, but divide into age categories if you like. Design a birdhouse for William Shakesbird, Walter Pidgeon, Anne Morrow Lindbird, Avian Gardner, Woodpecker Guthrie, Ernest Hummingway, etc. Offer to "Lend a Birdhouse-Maker" — a program for retired people to come to other people's homes, advise on birdhouses and build a birdhouse for a fee to be split between library and birdhouse-maker.

World of Sports. Paint a basketball, softball, volley ball, golf ball, tennis ball as a globe — as detailed or stylized as you wish. Get teenagers to do them in teams, each team taking a kind of ball. Use in display case. A fitting available in hardware stores, meant to support a closet pole, is a turned dish-like wood object, about 3–4″ in diameter. These can be painted and used as bases for the balls — all except golf balls. If possible, use a tee for them.

Raining in Sheets. Pull lengths of plastic wrap — the kind used in kitchens — taut, and staple to ceiling and floor of case, or even a room, to create the effect of a sheet of water or rain. Most effective if angled at about 70–80 degrees. If you use thin wrap, you may have to put a strip of masking tape along edge before stapling. You can increase the effect by slightly pleating or gathering the wrap at top and bottom, or by using double thicknesses. These should be lit at an angle from above. At the floor, where the water "hits" — make a puddle cut from bubble-pack plastic, small bubbles the best.

Barking — To catch the eye. Cover a variety of shapes with papier mâché or combed-plaster bark, and paint shades of brown. Milk jug, book, chair, phone. Put in window with a section of a tree. It means nothing, but catches the eye for a display on endangered trees, acid rain (see p199), dating trees by rings, what makes good firewood, chimney care.

Pillow and a Book. Check out a book and a pillow at lunchtime. Let people sit on the grass, as long as they are as careful of the grass as the books. Try to get inexpensive foam pillows donated, or at a discount from store. You'll need pillowcases too — people may donate. Lots of people would like to loll somewhere in the sun or shade in the middle of a hectic day, but find it uncomfortable.

What's So Funny? A small bulletin board or a standard can be decorated with a jester in cap and bell, or with Christmas-present colorful bells fastened to colored lengths of yarn along the bottom. Each week type out or print out a joke, bit of humorous verse, limerick or riddle. Put it by the exit, so people can exit smiling (if not chuckling).

Shelf Conscious? Headline for display of shelf of psychology books; or for photocopied articles on arranging bookshelves at home; or use to introduce a get acquainted with the library program — how to find your way around.

Fortune Bookie. A large cardboard book, perhaps made from one of those office supply shelf boxes that are made to look like books, with a hole large enough to admit a hand. Fill with one-line quotes or aphorisms. You can type them up on regular paper, have photocopied on colored paper, then cut in paper cutter into strips. Do 100 quotes in 2 or 3 hours and make 5 copies of each.

Bathroom Reading. For those of you who missed it, *Psychology Today*, December 1982, reported a study conducted in the lavatories of a college dorm. Posters showing how to administer CPR were put up inside the doors of bathroom stalls. Students from a postered dorm did better than from a posterless dorm, but researchers said that it was a technique that worked best to reinforce previous learning. Still, it is the kind of information that can be shown partly in illustrations, like the Heimlich Manuever for victims of choking, and it might be worthwhile putting such posters up inside the stalls in your bathrooms.

Income Taxes. Set up a tax display — books on filling out forms, saving taxes, latest wrinkles — near your photocopier, starting March 1.

Seurat Is to the Point. Paint backdrops, or cut-out standing forms such as trees or umbrella-ed, long-skirted women, à la French Impressionist Seurat. That is, with dots of color. Faces get mostly skin tones with pale blue or green shadow dots and white highlights. Even the brown trunks of trees get purple shadows.

Bus Messages. In New York City, a simple and amusing advertising/public service message appears on many city buses. Called the "Streetfair

Journal, The Magazine of the Rider," it uses one-line quips and bits of sometimes humorous advice — some of the best, I'm happy to say, are signed by "Aunt Linda." Adapt for a library campaign to broaden awareness. Quotes from ardent library fans and users; local celebrities and sports figures; quotes from new books designed to pique interest; facts about library holdings deemed of interest or use to the public who may not be using the library.

Grown-Ups. Provide a bulletin board for children to air their troubles with adults. (Note Stephen Greene Press' 1971 book by Russel Hamilton and Stephanie Greene entitled *What Bothers Us About Grownups, a Report Card on Adults by Children*.) Distribute questionnaires to children who frequent the library — perhaps give them a chance to air difficulties they have in using the library and dealing with adult librarians and patrons.

Games from the Past. Combine a display on the artifacts of games such as jacks, marbles, top-spinning, hoop-rolling, badminton, croquet, etc. (all of which survive in the 1980s, though not widely), with demonstrations, tournaments, even inter- and intramural competitions. For a marbles demonstration, it would be nice to do it the old way — on dirt. Using a length of garden hose taped with metallic gaffer's or duct tape to the floor, and filled with tightly packed dirt, you can set up a viable and realistic place for marbles. The circle should be between 9′ and 10′ across, and of course should be on a tile or other impervious surface. Half sand, half dirt, dampened and packed down, works well.

Community Leaders' Choices. Obtain photographs, preferably showing the various leaders reading, along with a short list — 3 to 5 titles — of preferred and recommended reading, books, offbeat journals or magazines. Newspapers should not be included — in a 2-newspaper town, or a strongly partisan newspaper town, this could get too political.

Help the Authors. Take partial paragraphs from current bestsellers or classics, and invite patrons to write the last sentence. Select the 25 to 50 best and put up a display.

Unexpected Color. Very large photostatic blowups of illustrations, which can be photographs, tone illustrations or bl/wh drawings in line, make effective backgrounds for floor displays — especially made up as suspended panels, or even folded screens, or are good in the back of cases and windows, or made up as posters. One very graphic and effective way to add color (color blowups themselves are usually prohibitively expensive) is to color by hand just one element or object. This is best done in an unexpected way, in an offbeat color, even in a surrealist way, to point up what may be the most important — even though smallest or obscure — element. A street scene, with a small dog: color the dog blue. A park scene, with a pigeon: color the pigeon brilliantly, like a parrot, with fanciful plumage and tail. A family group: color one face bright

red — anger? apoplexy? Broad-nib felt markers or the extremely con-
centrated Dr. Martin's watercolors are good for coloring on photographic or photostatic papers. To color, try for broad strokes that go
from one margin of the object to the other, even leaving streaks and
overlaps. Going back over the color tends to look fussy and messy.
Another way to color is to use sheets of self-stick plastic film, which
comes in various sheet sizes and many colors. It is virtually transparent. Lay down without bubbles (small bubbles can be pierced with a pin
point and will then smooth out); use an X-Acto™ razor knife to cut
around the edges of the object to be colored; remove excess margin
film; rub film down smoothly over object in picture. One maker of this
film is PANTONE® Color Letrafilm, by Letraset — the company that does
self-adhesive typefaces to be transferred with a special tool or a ballpoint pen to paper.

Triptychs and Diptychs. Many librarians faced with doing displays say that
one of their major problems is having only one huge bulletin board, on
one wall. Wall space is valuable, and perhaps better used for books,
although it is arguable that people have to have their attention at-
tracted to those books. Anyway, one solution to the vast steppes of an
arid bulletin board is to divide it into three parts or two parts. You can
use a strip of wood lath, painted to match the frame of the bulletin
board, or painted black or a bright color to further set off the divisions.
The three or two parts can become autonomous if you like, or each part
can somehow relate — by the style of lettering, type of headline, general
subject — to each other. This is how murals are often designed, because
they must fit onto walls divided by architectural elements ranging from
doors and windows to niches and columns.

Classifieds. Try running a weekly, inexpensive classified in the local news-
paper(s). During the spring and summer, when yardsales or garage
sales are popular, put one in reading "Bought a bargain? Come to the
library Saturday afternoons to find out what it's worth in our Collectibles Department." Or have a show-and-tell of best buys for the
month. Or offer a pair of afternoon or evening seminars in the spring,
and again in late summer, for people who want to have a yard sale but
don't know the first thing. There are a few books on the subject; a short
slide show could easily be made up quickly by a venturesome, bargain-
hunting staffer or volunteer; and you could have a panel of 2 or 3
speakers, with questions from the audience. Use it as a prelude to a
Friends of the Library garage sale.

What Else Is There? Some people think of the library as only a place to get
the latest mystery novel, or the latest poetry journal, or the latest
biography of a scientist. Remind them that the many collections of the
library — some of which may be housed in other buildings/branches —
are interrelated. Display a biography with a book on using the

microscope, a science magazine, and something on a subject revealed in the biography to be a favorite of the biographee — sailing, or needlepoint, or watching frogs. Handout booklists should also be prepared this way. Try to find the relatedness between things, not the unrelatedness. This is what education is supposed to do for people: show them how things are connected. Get out Jacob Bronowski's *Connections*, and use it as the basis for a long series of network displays.

How a _____ Is Born. For this year-long series, develop a border design for a bulletin board or a backdrop for one case or a window, that will have simple shapes of a wide range of things and beings that can be covered in the displays. **Star**: this could be an interesting combined display — on star performers and on celestial objects; **Book**: showing how a book is created, including a manuscript, a camera, galleys, blue and red pencils, bindings, slipcases. If there is a fine binder in your town, ask for a demonstration — even the simplest kind is interesting. Have a demonstration of paper marbleizing — maybe even sell marbleized sheets to benefit the library. With supervision, and assistance, and a nominal fee to pay for the photocopies, allow people to create their own books — up to 16 pages, with a heavy paper cover, stapled or handsewn. **Oak Tree**: plant a number of acorns, especially the ones old enough to have sprouted and begun to root, because you'll know they're viable, and watch them grow. Or do a bulletin board on germination or hybridization or grafting. **Piglet**: Everyone loves piglets. Pig embryos are pictured in many books, so it isn't hard to find material. Invite a portrait contest, if you live in a farm area, of baby pigs. **Idea**: books on inventions and/or artists.

Dusty Tomes: Exciting Times. Display on collecting old books. Most people believe — and for this we can bless their hearts because books *are* precious — that any old book is worth a lot of money. The idea of saving an old book is a valuable one to foster, as is the notion that a book is to be revered. But according to antiquarian bookmen and collectors, most books that turn up in attics and basements are not valuable antiques. People would find it interesting to find out how to look up titles in *Book Prices Current*, or how to read *AB Bookman's Weekly*, how to use other library references to check the value of books. There is a large body of literature that would appeal to the armchair antiquarian too — books on the exciting searches and finds of 18th, 19th and 20th century antiquarian bookstores all over the country. Related to this would be a seminar on caring for home libraries, no matter what size or what value, and how to combat silverfish, mildew and bookworms.

Bowser Browses. Dog tales, puppy-care books, famous dogs or dogs of the famous. Collections of dog tags — yep! many people collect them. Or a display of dog art, or children's art of their pets.

Freeze Frieze. Icicles sprayed on the glass, cut from semi-translucent plastic (including milk jugs) — use them in the hottest part of summer to look cool. Remember how shops lucky enough to have air-conditioning, 30 years ago or so, would have icicles painted on a sign that bragged how "cool inside" it was?

Tips & Hints of the Month. Lots of problems are solvable with help from books and/or other people's suggestions. Pose a problem in big type, such as **How to Make Fleas Flee, How I Quit Smoking, How to Make Cheap Bookcases, How to Rainproof Good Shoes, How to Feed an Old Cat, How to Make Indoor Plants Bloom**, etc. Put up a few photocopies of solutions found in books; invite the public to contribute their solutions. Keep up the entire month. Type out all contributed answers, and selected short quotes from the books — with full credit for all. This makes a nice handout.

Ten Years Ago This Week, or 25 Years Ago This Year, or Last Year on This Day. Use *Facts on File* to come up with something unusual. This makes a good opener for a 5-minute radio show, and a take-off point for something to talk about.

Nutty Professors, Experts and Wacky Authors. Make up your own aphorisms and "famous" sayings, using real ones and putting in sound-alike words having to do with books, learning, publishing, etc. Sign with punned names. "Our clothes conceal our blemishes; our books reveal our prejudices." — *Melvil Pfui*. "Books are stray words that have been given a good home." — *Olden Runes*. "Though libraries have a thousand books, each is the only one." — *B.O. Wolfe*. "The tongue of the reader reveals what is on the mind of the writer." — *Juan Derrin Minstrall*. "The universe of learning is always unfinished ... and every student carries his own frontier." — *R.S. Tottle*. "The censor is one kind of murderer." — *James Rejoice*. "When a book has no other virtues, a period at the end can be considered one." — *A. Paige Turner*. "Knowledge is like the plank to the bridge; the wider and thicker it is, the more weight it will carry." — *Thoreau Lee Read*. "A book with a thousand readers has a thousand messages." — *Bess Celler*. "Better a book that says 'I wonder' than a book that lies." — *Ralph Quarto Emerson*. "The library is a 'seat of learning' because learning requires a talent for sitting." — *Throwa Book Attem*. "You can derive a lot of interest from principles." — *George Henry*. "The worst prophet of the future is a closed book looked at by a closed mind." — *Novella N. Binding*. "Every word is gain, and gain is gain, however small." — *Chap Tand Versa*.

Events & Publicity

We're in a Pickle. Delicatessans, and probably restaurants, have huge glass jars with screw-on lids, with pickles. The jars get thrown out when the last pickle is gone. Get several, soak with a solution of baking soda and water. Create large pickle labels with green pickles and the motto "We're in a pickle – the library needs your contributions." Cut slot in each lid for coins and bills. In addition, make up bookmarks shaped like pickles, put up posters in cooperating delis and restaurants, sell homemade pickles, have a sandwiches 'n' pickles fund raiser dinner – formal but with a variety of sandwich fixin's and donated pickles.

Children's Art Show. Everyone loves to see children's art, especially if the proud artists are there to show off and explain their pictures. Get the cooperation of town's art teachers. Pick a theme – perhaps "What Our Library Will Look Like in a Hundred Years" – or ask them to draw a scene from their favorite book. Pictures can be hung with clothespins from lines strung along walls or criss-crossing a space in the center court.

Oh, You Doll! Doll-collecting is, according to whom you hear, either first, second or third in popularity with collectors. The other two fields are stamps and coins. Dolls of all sizes appeal to people and artists of all sizes and ages. Have a doll-making or doll-repairing demonstration or workshop all day long, including a special section for young children. Display an antique doll collection, or a dolls-from-many-lands collection, or sponsor a contest to create dolls of literary figures – characters or authors. Connect this series of events to your costume collection and theater collection.

What's Cooking? Interest in cookery and cookbooks never dies down. No one knows this as well as the librarian, who must keep up with the cookbook collection, as if thousands of them didn't already exist. Keep a large size file box, divided up like cookbooks into Vegetables, Bread, Cookies, Cake, Meats, Chicken, Salads, etc., with 5×7 cards stamped with the library's name on which patrons can copy out their favorite recipes. These cards can be copied by hand by other patrons or photocopied. You will find that a good proportion of "favorite" recipes are straight out of a published cookbook. Urge recipe contributors to credit their sources; in addition, don't count on creating a library fund-raising cookbook from these collected recipes, unless each is re-written completely. Perhaps if you stress how important copyright law is, everyone will be very careful. There are a number of publishers who do special spiral-bound cookbook publishing for communities and charities. They often provide color divider pages and covers, but you may create your own – even black and white can be effective. (And see the chapter in this book on Clip Art for ideas on how to create a cook-book.) One company, used by hundreds of fund-raising organizations, will send you their interesting brochure, samples, and paper samples: Write Wayne J. Dankert, WALTER'S CO., RFD #4, Waseca, MN 56093.

Pet Shows. Unusual pets may draw the most interest. See if you can round up a snake owner, tarantula owner, ferret owner, and have them bring their pets and paraphernalia, plus anything extra interesting, such as shed skins. By the way, tarantulas shed their furry back and orange skins — the funniest-looking fur coats you ever saw, and after a few minutes of steeling yourself, you may even be able to touch one ... a skin, not the spider. Bees have just been declared pets in parts of Virginia; part of the argument that won them that status was that a fence will tend to keep a bee in your yard just as it will a dog! A pet show of any kind — even of cats and/or dogs — is the perfect time to really help the local and national humane societies and ASPCAs and other shelters press home their urgent messages: wild animals do not make good pets and are often illegal pets; and often the "miracle of birth" leads to the tragedy of death. We just plain have too many dogs and cats for all of them to have happy homes. The third message is that baby ducks and chickens and rabbits may be awfully lovable and cute, but interest wanes in a few weeks or months, the animal may be un-suitable for living indoors, and what person of conscience would want to turn a pet into a meal?

Bring a Friend. Urge patrons, particularly those in difficult-to-reach groups such as teenagers, business people, farmers, new immigrants, to bring in as many friends as they can to introduce to the joys and satisfactions of the library. Have a contest every quarter to see who can sign up and convince the most friends or acquaintance. Be prepared to meet the needs of such groups before you urge them to come to the library. Pair a patron with a librarian to take a tour around. What the librarian will think to point out as a wonder or point of pride may be quite different from what a special patron will focus on.

Scrabble™ Tournaments. This can be played with individuals who stay with a series of games for the duration, or — to include more people — some-thing like tag teams of 4 people. What the Scrabble people need to do is find a way to enlarge the board and increase the number of tiles, so that games could last longer. They'd have to come up with a way to keep those triple word score squares at the edge at a reasonable dis-tance from the center, so that you wouldn't have to wait forever to get a triple word score.

Biweekly Museums. NYC has a Dog Museum of America, with collections and exhibitions of all manner of dog items. Your library could set aside one large case or window for a changing museum — this is a good one for volunteers and representatives of groups, trades and professions outside the library to be in charge of, because it will bring people in from outside. Making it biweekly gives you 26 museums a year, some of which could become travelling exhibits set up later either at branch libraries or at headquarters for the various groups and trades. The museums should be a combination of library materials, artifacts, demonstrations or tours, keepsakes and booklists. One exhibit at the Dog Museum was called "D" is for Dog, and comprised alphabet books, and a giveaway poster that could be folded into a 16-page booklet imitation of an alphabet book. There was also a teacher's kit to show how to encourage children to create their own alphabet books. Taking alphabet books as a theme, each of your 26 museums could be set up that way. An alphabet border or backdrop could remain constant throughout the year, with facsimile or imitation alphabet blocks used to display objects. At the end of the year, create a scrapbook of photos and photocopies of any caption materials, plus examples of any printed giveaways.

Cable TV. Scores of new local cable TV channels (and FM radio stations) are opening up. Now's the time to write up a proposal for a once-a-week storytelling or puppet show program for children, to be taped at the library, using staff or volunteer story tellers, who are probably already busy at work for a limited number of children. Tape another half hour adult show, which could range from readings of classic stories or mysteries, to a narrated exploration of a subject in pictures to be found at the library.

Coloring Posters. Simple black and white line drawing posters, preferably 11 × 17 rather than 8½ × 11, can be easily and cheaply reproduced on ordinary photocopy paper, passed out by the hundreds to school children for coloring and posting — in schools, neighborhood stores, beauty parlors and barber shops, inserted into menus of local restaurants, taped inside a back window of the family's car, passed out at company picnics or church suppers. The children get a kick out of coloring posters advertising the library; adults will admire the efforts and perhaps be moved to see what all the fuss is about. Art from clip art books can be used, and the poster should advertise a particular kind of adult or juvenile service or event.

Lunchtime Introductions. For preliminaries, send out information to local businesses, plants, meeting places, outlining a program to follow the next month on "What the Library Can Do for You." You'll need a quick-witted staffer, possibly a reference librarian, who is used to fielding questions on a wide variety of subjects, who can introduce the library's particular and general services to a special audience. If it's the police precinct — the librarian can talk about the collections involving psychology, classic crime detection, library-sponsored youth

programs and job counseling, census materials, second-language tapes
and books, etc. If it's an electronics plant — talk about the range of current periodicals and journals (many of them too expensive for individuals to subscribe to), histories of industry pioneers, self-improve-
ment books and books on new styles of worker/management relations, books on gardening — to start a company garden, exercise to
counteract stress books, etc. Bring a handout of some kind, that includes a very special personal invitation to each person. Include that
person's family and friends; arrange an openhouse to give them a tour
of the facilities. Sometimes it seems that inertia keeps people from ever
entering the library. There's another, more important reason: unease
and shyness. Think about it. Don't you feel ill at ease and lost when
you enter a supermarket or department store you've never been in
before? What are the house rules, how do you behave, where *is* everything?

Borrow a Reader/Lend a Listener. Lots of people need someone to talk to,
and it is possible that the library could establish a roster of people ex-
perienced in various fields (excluding legal and medical) who could be
sympathetic and helpful listeners. Set up along the lines of the programs that match retired business people with inner city people who
wish to start businesses. A scrapbook with photos and resumes of the
available listeners would be available. Listeners as well as the borrowers of an ear should be screened to some extent.

Semi-invalids, stay-at-homes, people in hospital, lonely people,
people with poor eyesight, would benefit from a weekly reader. Volunteer readers, who should have a fluent reading style, could include
foreign language readers. They would be available once a week or more
often if possible to go to private homes, nursing homes or hospitals to
read aloud, and should be willing to read what the "borrower/listener"
selects from a list of general types of selections. This program might be
particularly effective in a hospital setting. Many people are hospi-
talized some distance from home, and have few if any visitors. If group
readings were done, follow the example of Norman Cousins and read
light, upbeat materials that will improve morale.

Newcomers to Town. Reach out to newcomers by sending flyers out weekly,
biweekly or monthly either to "resident" or to a list of known pur-
chasers of new homes. Such a list could be compiled from the newspaper or from a real estate group. Broaden the program to include
apartment renters, by inviting building owners or managers to a special
reception at the library (many of them may not be patrons either) to
make them feel in partnership with the library in extending the library's
welcome to newcomers. A good booklist to accompany such mailings
and events would include books on the move itself and the new community, as well as maps, lists of organizations open to all new

residents, etc. If illustrated, this booklist should have people of all races and ages represented.

Local History on Tape. Set up a program, perhaps administered by volunteers interested in local history, or a retired local historian, to record the stories of residents who can share the kinds of experiences that make up a complete picture of your community. Elderly people, long-time tradespeople, retired firefighters and policemen – all could contribute their recollections of events and people of the community. The view doesn't have to be global or based on 50 years of experiences; a single major fire, a single encounter with a local legend, a recollection of a barn-raising or a presidential whistle stop – all add up. Set up a time, every day if possible, so that people could make appointments to come to the library. At other times, the person in charge could make visits to homebound residents. Each interested person, some of whom may be illiterate, should understand what sort of thing they might talk about, what kinds of followup questions they might be asked, and what kinds of ephemera or memorabilia they might be encouraged to donate to the library. You can use a tape recorder, which is unobtrusive; plus a video camera, if the library can get one (the price keeps getting lower and lower); and a Polaroid or other instant camera to get a picture of the person contributing to the local history collection. Some people need to be asked questions, others need only to be wound up and started. Reminiscences of buildings, new bridges, schooldays, parades, the first telephone, baseball teams, desegregation – all these are valued subjects for interviews. The next question is whether or not to edit tapes to create stories on specific subjects, or to index each tape. Transcription is a terrible expense of time and money, but duplicate tapes are not, and should be considered – at least for the most revealing and interesting ones.

The intimate view of local history resulting from these interviews would be a good basis for a cable TV show, as described above.

Corporate Cooperation. Establish personal connections to company librarians and historians, as well as chief executive officers, managers and department heads to make them feel part of the library's large farmily. They are in a position to suggest the library as a source of information or help to all the corporate employees. Send out a fact sheet or library annual report to inhouse newsletter editors, asking for their cooperation in publicizing the library. Observe the pecking order – many corporations are very tightly structured, and the chain of command is observed before practically anything is done.

Press Releases. Just as the library is divided into departments – Art, Business, Genealogy, Sci-Tech – so is the newspaper, although sometimes one reporter does articles in several fields. Set up within the library a definite schedule for issuing press releases. These can be of varying degrees of newsworthiness. A dependable source of short, interesting fillers would be welcome to most local newspapers, so one kind of press release that you send out frequently and regularly would report on a new acquisition of topical interest, an odd occurrence or question from the public. Rotate press releases from the library's various departments. Encourage department heads and staffers to keep a file of p-slips on which they can jot down anything that might be incorporated in a press release.

This Is the Way.... Do a series of skits and displays featuring ethnic dance, music, costume, cookery, folklore, herbalism, language. These can be scheduled around historic dates of significance to the particular group, or to something like Black History Month, which could feature four programs — two African cultures, a Caribbean culture, an American sub-culture such as the world of jazz or doo-wap or tap. This series is primarily cultural events, but the same idea could be adapted to various professions — "This is the way we do our work. These are the special clothes we wear, our special mask, the tools we use, the lingo we employ in everyday work, the way we spend our lunch hour."

Networking Parties at the Library. Invite leaders in various businesses and professions to be co-hosts with the library, the guests to be young people looking for a career, people looking to advance or change their careers, people returning to the workforce. Could be all on one night, like career night at highschool, with booths set up. Among the people to invite as co-hosts: representatives from the mechanical and building trades including skilled tradespeople and suppliers and representatives from the unions; TV and radio people — including technician, cameraperson, disk jockey, newscaster; police and firefighters; politicians; teachers; little theater set designer; church choir director; nurse; paramedical and paralegal representatives; craftsperson; freelance writer; etc.

Writers' Hotline. In Washington, there's a group of professors of English called "Grammarphone," who are called by people in the White House and the Congress for advice in writing speeches, press releases, and reports. According to an article in the *Baltimore Sun*, January 18, 1983, Grammarphone is one of several "such university-based services in the country." Why not open such a service at the library; most libraries have been serving that function for years anyway. If your town is sizeable enough, you may be able to get subscribers to the service, companies and/or individuals willing to make an annual contribution. Public libraries are in the odd position of having to (and wanting to) provide as much information as they can, free of charge, but being unrewarded and underpaid for this service. The dependency of many companies — ranging from scientific labs to publishing firms — on telephone reference is staggering, and many of these profit-oriented firms do not make contributions — over and above the tiny tax alottment of individuals working there — to the library. Many such firms do not even send one of their paid employees to do the research; they tie up library phones and personnel, sometimes asking for a call back on the requested data. For shame!

Newsletters. One of the most important tools a library can use to reach out is a newsletter (see pages 193-197). It can be as short as one page, closely typed, or as long as 8 pages. Two to 4 pages are probably the best — not too long to write or read, but long enough for a variety of news notes and messages. The subject matter can range over a wide area; for example, the Plainedge (New York) Public Library started publishing a monthly for single parents, plus one in cooperation with the local school system. Some newsletters are intended more for staffers and librarians in other towns than for the general public. Newsletters are expensive and therefore some libraries are reluctant to start one, only to have to quit if the expense gets too great. Newsletters can be used to attract new "customers" for the library, in which case mailing only to library card holders is beside the point, or they can be used to raise funds and increase usage, in which case they can be sent to users and nonusers. In the business world, there are essentially two kinds of newsletters — those that give very timely and very expensive information/advice to the select few able or willing to pay for this service, and the kind that is meant to act as a vehicle for selling goods. The latter kind is quite interesting to study. The information in it may or may not be dated or timely — even if it's called "news." Much of the material may be news in the sense that it's new to the person reading it; it may in fact be material from 100 or 500 years ago. The mood and feeling of insidership that this type of newsletter builds in its readership creates a climate and a readiness for selling and buying related goods. For the library, such a newsletter can sell the services and the institution of the library, but it can also be used to sell stationery, books, bumper stickers, tee-shirts, tote bags, stickers, blank books, pencils imprinted with the library's name, limited edition posters from pictures in the library's collection, etc. It can also be used to sell volunteerism, membership in Friends organizations, and contributions to fund special buying or building programs, and to solicit estate gifts.

Newsletters can be distributed in bank lobbies, at schools and universities, at the check-out at the library itself, through the mail, or in neighborhood drives. (Remember that it is illegal to put an unstamped item in a mailbox. You may get permission from the local newspapers to put in the newspaper box, or you can put behind the screen door or in apartment lobbies.)

Many books are available on editing and publishing newsletters. Two good ones are *Success in Newsletter Publishing; A Practical*

Guide, by Frederick D. Goss, Washington, DC: Newsletter Association of America, 1982, which is quite technical on some aspects, but will help you create a professional level; and *Editing Your Newsletter: A Guide to Writing, Design and Production*, by Mark Beach, Portland, OR: Coast to Coast Books, 1983, which includes many full-page examples from real newsletters, as well as illustrative material on doing layouts, preparing photographs for reproduction, etc. If you can buy only one, buy Mark Beach's book. A booklist is available from Ross Book Service, Box 12093, Seminary Post Office, Alexandria, VA 22304, called "Tools of the Trade." It will be of great help in getting the books you need to write and publish a newsletter.

Fast Food Tray Liners. This can be approached at the local level, but it would be a great idea for A.L.A. too. Ask the local McDonald's (well-known for their corporate attitude toward charity and community involvement) or other fast food outlet to print tray liners with a library message. If you want to try it, you may be able to persuade a lot of local restaurants and fast food outlets to include a printed library message on their placemats or tray liners—perhaps something like "If you like to read, but you've read this placemat at least 10 times, why not visit your public library, where you can feast to your heart's content on current magazines, books and newspapers." Or, "If you feed to live, and live to read—come to the library for a second course." Etc., etc.

Bedtime Stories. Between 10 and midnight, for 15 minutes, try to get a weekly radio program for the library. This is when most people are in bed preparing for sleep, or winding up their day and ready to relax. A few book reviews, with selected reading from the books, a guest to talk about a local bestseller, or reading from books are all possible programs. The station may want to tape a month's programs all at once. The essentials are a fairly low-pitched mellifluous voice, terrific diction, and a comforting, friendly, expressive attitude that will make listeners feel they have a friend at the library.

Teddy Bear Story Time. Have children bring their own bears (but have a number of temporary adoptable bears too) to a weekly story time. Or make it any kind of stuffed animal or doll. Encourage the children to read to their bears or dolls at home, or to ask their parent to do so.

Word Games Anonymous. Collect a coterie of people who love to play word games—from Fictionary to Anagrams—and who would like to learn more games and play the ones they know more often. If the library has room, hold such games, for from 4 to 8 people, at the library. Or establish proxy-libraries in other spaces, and hang up your temporary **Library in Session—Word Games Played Here** shingle. Collect a set of books useful for word gamers—dictionaries, special Scrabble dictionaries, etc.

Anniversaries. For upcoming 50th or 100th library anniversaries, sponsor a contest for children to draw and describe what the library will look like, what it will lend, and to whom it will lend, in another 50 or 100 years. Drawings and brief excerpts from descriptions can be used handsomely in a special anniversary publication. That's a good opportunity to really spread the word about the library; everyone loves anniversary celebrations. Perhaps anniversary cakes can be made and donated by local bakeries; anniversary bookmarks printed and donated by local printers; a song composed and performed by local musicians.

Wrap It Up. Gift wrap demonstrations, perhaps with books on gift wrap and craft demonstrations — collage and photocopier techniques for creating wraps and cards, etc.

Kites. Kitemaking demonstration, with a display of kites in central court, strung from the ceiling. Sponsor a kite-flying contest, with kite-flying teams getting pledges to go to library.

Monetary Gift Catalog. Brown University alumni received something interesting in April 1981 — a full-color "Spring Gift Catalogue" that offered gift opportunities ranging in value from $10 to $10-million. It solicited contributions to various funds, foundations, endowments and real estate at the university. A library could do this, though not so grandly and in color, by creating a faux-catalogue. The gifts being solicited could be illustrated with clip art.

Eat and Fund. Universities and libraries have had fundraisers based on food for some time. One university a few years ago had a realistic 14th century banquet, with jesters; another reenacted the inaugural dinner given for George Washington. Recently, the New York Public Library sponsored a number of supper parties, given by socialites around the city, and subscribed to by a small number of guests. Some were theme suppers. The evening wound up at the library itself. Similar events can be tried by any community — even those who prefer not to depend on socialites for their support. An article in *Money*, December 1982, is full of fund-raising ideas. One described in the article is a "celebrity cook-off, where a dozen notables whipped up their favorite dishes at cooking stations paid for by businesses." Every community has its notables — people whom everyone reads about in the newspaper, but rarely lays eyes on: the mayor, the chief of police, the newspaper's managing editor, the library's director, the chief surgeon at the hospital, the star basketball player at the college, the housewife who was once Queen for a Day, the midnight disk jockey, the gospel choir members, the airplane instructor, etc.

Display and Promotion Calendar
With Suggested Themes and Projects

The following long list of annotated dates is meant to indicate the wide range of subjects under your purview, and to suggest a simple technique for finding a subject for promotion. It is in no way complete — many days are left out altogether. But using the key word or fact about an historical event is the clue to creating a display. Some events are fixed for a particular date; others move around — the first Sunday, the week that includes Eleanor Roosevelt's birthday, the third Monday after a full moon, etc.

January

1 Rose, Orange & Sugar Bowl football games played. Offer an alternative: Book Bowl Game — with a display of sports books or any other kind. Reading is a quiet sport, but everyone's a winner.

3 J.R.R. Tolkien born, 1892. Best known for his Hobbits, Tolkien wrote many other things. *Leaf by Niggle* is a wonderful short novella; adapt a leaf display, with large paper leaves, and perhaps include García Márquez's novella *Leaf Storm*.

4 Jacob Grimm, one of the 2 German fairy-telling brothers, born, 1785. Readings from Grimm, Andersen or modern fabulists. Grimm is grim ... rereading a few today, I'm not sure many people would want young children to hear them. An adult study group could have a great seminar on *The Frog-King* or other Freud-fraught fables. For kids, introduce the silly, funny fairy tales by Monty Pythoner Terry Jones.

4 Louis Braille born, 1809. Emphasize your mail-a-book service to the blind; large-type books; recorded books; and any other services for the people with impaired sight. Get someone to come speak about the opportunity to record for the blind. A book read aloud on successive Wednesdays, say, to a group of sight-impaired people would have a

more enlivening sociable effect than if the same book were listened to at home, alone.

5 George Washington Carver Day — he died on this day in 1943. Ingenuity in American agriculture; the African background of peanuts — goobers; have a peanut and/or sweet potato recipe contest and put together in a fund-raising booklet, or hold a bake-off of sweet 'tater pies, and then a pay-for-a-piece party.

6 Sherlock Holmes' birthday. Start a mystery book discussion group. Bring mystery book display up near checkout, featuring works of Conan Doyle. "It's not a mystery at the library" — a campaign to show nonusers how easy it is to find out the answers to mysteries.

11 Alexander Hamilton, first Secretary of the Treasury, born, 1757. Books on planning finances, investing. A talk by a local securities broker or a panel of them, on investment opportunities. Start a contribution drive for the library.

12 The 1st American museum opened, in Charleston, SC, 1773. Exhibit objects of library history; do prehistoric reptile children's exhibit (a reconstructed skeleton was featured at Charleston); with a large-scale cardboard, plywood or foam board skeleton. Exchange tours and flyers, and combine publicity forces with local museum.

13 Horatio Alger born, 1834. Rising above hard times; investment books, with visiting lecturers. Entrepreneurship seminar, with local people who have secrets to share. Now's a good time to bring out an array of government documents, which most people don't know exist.

13 Stephen Foster Memorial Day — he died on this day in 1864. Relate Foster's song, "My Old Kentucky Home" to the "Home Sweet Home" motto — what home means; decorating, building or restoring; have a singalong, with banjoist. Have an art exhibit showing how aspects of American life are described in popular songs — 19th century to the present. (Mark Sullivan's Our Times series is filled with song information, as are many old issues of "American Heritage.")

14 Albert Schweitzer, humanitarian, philosopher, physician, born, 1875. Sponsor panel discussion on altruism, with ethics professor, church representatives, fire chief, and perhaps someone from local hospital ethics committee.

15 Martin Luther King, Jr., born, 1929. Civil rights — what progress we've made, what erosions have taken place; put up large-type photostat of his "I have a dream" speech; films on the brotherhood of all people.

17 St. Anthony's Day. Blessing of the Animals. Sponsor talk by humane or ASPCA society rep on how to increase awareness. Hold public forum on the blessings and health benefits animals bestow on us. Hold a pet-blessing ceremony for children and adults and make it ecumenical, perhaps with a specially-written blessing from the writings of a well-known animal lover. Cosponsor a pet adoption display with local pet

humane society, with a booklist on animal care and human respon-
sibilites. (See May 3 in this calendar). Combine with the ethics
programming.

17 Benjamin Franklin born, 1706. Invention; inspiration for progress;
electrical repair books — perhaps a lamp-repair demonstration; energy-
saving materials and talk by local utilities spokesperson. Or do a display
covering printing to word processing — with a practical demonstration.

19 Edgar Allan Poe born, 1809. Have a gold bug festival and let everyone
make the most outlandish gold bug they can from scrap and found
materials. Have a spooky reading of *The Pit and the Pendulum*, and
create an 8' pendulum to swing back and forth behind the reader. Have
a wine-tasting party and read *The Cask of Amontillado*. Sponsor a
mystery readers' hotline bulletin board, with printed info cards people
can fill out and post to recommend their favorites and new discoveries.
(See January 6.)

20 Basketball played the first time, 1892, in Springfield, Massachusetts.
Feature basketball players' biographies; sell popcorn balls at a game between local sports writers and newscasters and librarians, and raise
money for library. Show tapes of basketball games. Hold a dribbling
contest right in the library, with penny pledges for every bounce.

21 Count Basie recorded his signature tune "One o'Clock Jump." Fill a
small case with ticking alarm clocks and a pair of men's and women's
dancing shoes.

22 In 1982, 75% of America was snow-covered. Throw a snowflake party,
with sherbets and ice creams, and cut-out snowflakes to fasten to
ice cream sticks. Sign up volunteers to shovel library snow; sign up
others to pick up and return book, select and check out new ones, for
homebound or snow-hampered people.

23 National Handwriting Day — also John Hancock's birthday in 1737. Invite reps from local art stores to do demonstrations and perhaps sell
(with some percentage going to library) lettering pens, ink and paper.
Or get paper from odd lots donated by printer or stationer's. Borrow a
wheeled chalk board from school for chalk demonstration. Create an
old-style, browned-around-the-edges poster "Sign Your John Hancock
Here" — several of them as keepsakes for local history division. Display
on collecting autographs or letters, or the ancient graffiti impulse.
Feature an upbeat handwriting analysis expert — $1.00 for each, to go in-
to library fund.

25 Nation's first transcontinental phone line opened, 1915. Sponsor forum
with reps from local Bell company plus various long-distance services
available in your community. Do flyer on library's phone book collection. Have kids make waxed string and tin can phones.

27 Wolfgang Amadeus Mozart born, 1756. Have a tape/record concert at
lunch time. Invite children to bring in toy pianos, xylophones, or other

toy euphonious instruments for an impromptu ensemble concert. *Note*: Jerome Kern was born this day, 1885, and Arthur Rubenstein was born the 28th, 1886 (né "Artur," he Americanized it to "Arthur").

27 Anniversary of the Signing of the Vietnam Peace Pact. Books, etc., on veteran's problems; novels and plays on Vietnam; treaties in general.

27 Television first publicly demonstrated, in Scotland, 1926. Show videos of some really historic show; display books that have been made into TV mini-series or longer series. Have forum on TV violence, and the shaping of a whole new kind of world perception — everything takes place in 27 minutes from problem to solution.

28 The word "serendipity" coined by Horace Walpole, 1754. Do display explaining what serendipity means; have tour of stacks, with people allowed to take one book that they never expected to find, to study back upstairs.

28 Should be a full moon about now. Check paper. Show an old horror film; read werewolf tales. Have a community baying-at-the-moon concert with refreshments afterward and invitation to join the Friends group. Get a speaker to talk on "lunacy," and the relationship between strange behavior and the fully-waxed moon.

29 Comedian W.C. Fields (Claude William Dukenfield) born, 1880. Have a showing of some of his great films. Prepare a glossary of some of this great humorist's favorite expressions.

31 Ballerina Anna Pavlova born, 1885. (*Note*: ballerina Maria Tallchief born the 24th, 1925.) Ballet books, ballet music played at lunch time. Ballet books, ballet music played at lunch time. Ballet exercises demonstrated and participated in.

31 Zane Grey born, 1875. Western novels; evening of tall tales — read or told by the best local story tellers; exploitation of western lands; throw a zany, gray costume party and serve — oh, dear! — any gray food you can think of.

February

1 Black History Month begins. Prepare speakers' programs and an Afro-American culture display. Do printout of books on black history and pertinent biographies and prepare booklist.

1 National Freedom Day. If you haven't done it before, do a Freedom to Read display. Initiate letter-writing campaign direct to Congress and the President about the present threats to reading and intellectual freedoms. The day gets its name because the Justices of the Supreme Court sat first in 1790. Feature books on the Court or the Justices. Hold a forum about the next Supreme Court — what its tenor will be.

2, 5, 9   A trio of weather-climate dates. It's Groundhog Day the 2nd; America's first weatherman, John Jeffries, was born the 5th, 1745; the U.S. Weather Bureau established the 9th, 1870. Have a Weather Week, including booklists on weather forecasting, old almanacs; displays on industrialization's effect on climate, acid rain, books on weather-related disasters; demonstration of how to read the newspaper weather map; display of folkloric weather forecastings — from "red sky in the morning" to "birds going to bed early." Have a weather predicting contest; have people fill out a prepared form, giving predicted temperature at noon, description of clouds, wind velocity, etc. for one week from the day. Have a display of weathervanes, or start fund raising to buy a library weathervane.

4   Charles Lindbergh, aviator, born, 1902. (See May 20.)

4   Winter Olympics held first time in USA, 1932. Throw sledding/skating party, with a snug, warm reading of good short story back at the library. Show films on mountaineering, skiing, or champion skaters. Display borrowed antique skates or sleds; have a mitten knittin' fest, with shared, photocopied patterns.

4   USO founded, 1941. Arrange a special program for enlisted men and women in your area — a social hour, and introduce a special new service for them, or a booklist.

5   Baseball player Hank Aaron born, 1934, and

6   Babe Ruth born, 1895. If the skies are clear in your town, have an early baseball celebration. Do a booklist for armchair fans; a display on books with baseball themes. A display of stamps featuring baseball, from all over the world. (A 1984 Nicaraugan stamp featured Babe Ruth.)

7   The Beatles made their first American appearance, 1964, on the Ed Sullivan program. Beatles' music (now considered classic by just about everybody, no matter how odd and wild it seemed then); rock history; rock 'n' roll as poetry; a 25 year history of men's hairstyles.

8   Boy Scouts of America founded, 1910. Program for all Scouts, boys and girls and former Scouts; propose a public service project that local Scouts can take on around the library; push the reading badge.

12   Abraham Lincoln born, 1809, and

12   N.A.A.C.P. founded, 1909. Afro-American history; books and government serials on civil rights; Lincoln's Emancipation Proclamation; Lincoln the statesman, the humorist, the orator.

15, 19   Galileo Galilei born, 1564, on the 15th; Nicholas Copernicus born the 19th, 1473. Astronomy; space exploration (*note*: John Glenn orbited Earth three times on February 20, 1962); religion and science — the various damping and encouraging influences the church has had on science.

16 Film-maker Robert Flaherty born, 1884. Start a Thursday night Flaherty Film Festival, start with *Nanook of the North*. Have photo show of dogs in the snow.

18 Louis Comfort Tiffany — Mr. Art Nouveau — born, 1848. Is there a local antique show scheduled about now? Sponsor ½ day symposium on appraising, doing flea markets, buying antiques. Sign up local collectors for 6 months of case displays. Create a colored glass effect in a case or window using self-stick Pantone film (see materials list appendix).

21 *The New Yorker* magazine first published, 1925. Your library's *New Yorker* and other magazine collections make good displays — particularly old graphics as seen on covers. Short story collections or cartoons; E.B. White's essays/letters; Thurber stories/biographies; travelling to NYC from your town — guides and advice, including how to look up things in the NYTimes.

25 Constitutional Amendment XVI established Income Tax, 1913. April 15 isn't that far away — do up a tax preparedness checklist so people can feel they're making progress each week — things like Sort Bills, File Receipts, Collect W-9 forms, talk to Broker. Celebrate April 16 with tea party.

26 Grand Canyon became National Park, 1919. Materials on controversies surrounding exploitation of national parks, limiting tourism, raising fees, etc. Grandeurs of nature in photography; geology.

26 Fats Domino, "Blueberry Hill" rock 'n' roll star, born, 1928. R & R hasn't died at all. New music and dances — electric boogie, breaking, go-go, rapping — are today's folk music, street poetry. The library doesn't judge art forms, it helps preserve them. Sponsor a concert and performance by local kids, record it on video for the archives — no-one else may be doing it.

28 Final M*A*S*H episode aired, 1983. Start a community seminar (see January 27, February 4) where veterans can air their needs and feelings to people — many of whom may never have met a Vietnam veteran.

29 Leap ahead. Make propositions, resolutions, celebrations. "Make it Memorable — Propose in the Library" — pair up comfortable chairs, just for the day, in secluded nooks around the library. The library's a great place for a safe, comfortable romance.

Chinese New Year. Usually takes place in February. Play Chinese music; make a giant fortune cookie from thin foam padding (a diaper shape, pulled up and stapled shut) to fill with fortune slips or aphorisms. Have an "Aren't You Fortunate Fortune Cookie Stuffing party for volunteers. Hand out chart, with selection of natural history or aptly titled books for the specific year.

Rat	1924	1936	1948	1960	1972	1984
Ox	1925	1937	1949	1961	1973	1985
Tiger	1926	1938	1950	1962	1974	1986

Rabbit	1927	1939	1951	1963	1975	1987
Dragon	1928	1940	1952	1964	1976	1988
Snake	1929	1941	1953	1965	1977	1989
Horse	1930	1942	1954	1966	1978	1990
Sheep	1931	1943	1955	1967	1979	1991
Monkey	1932	1944	1956	1968	1980	1992
Bird	1933	1945	1957	1969	1981	1993
Dog	1934	1946	1958	1970	1982	1994
Boar	1935	1947	1959	1971	1983	1995

Chinese cookbooks, demonstration of doing *dim sum*, fundraiser at local Chinese restaurant.

March

1 Save Your Vision Week and Red Cross Month begin. Books for visually impaired; tips on how to read – the right way for your eyes; history of the Red Cross; demonstration of life-saving techniques.

2 First non-stop, round-the-world plane landed, Ft. Worth, TX, 1949. Vacation planning – do theme displays on other places. Do a "Travel at Home" plan for taking "trips" by reading library maps, travelogues, classic traveller's stories (Laurence Sterne's *Sentimental Journey*, for example). Film series: train trips, English villages (remember the funny *Green Man*?) or Miss Marple films; Mexico – from Louis Buñuel to Huston's *Treasure of the Sierra Madre*.

3 "The Star Spangled Banner" became national anthem, 1931. American flag; flags of all nations; examine words of anthem (many people object to "bombs bursting in air" as an unglorious vision for the nuclear age); sponsor a Library Anthem contest.

3 Inventor Alexander Graham Bell born, 1847. Thomas Alva Edison born the same year, February 11; that is when National Inventors Day is. Start a community local history research project to unveil any past or present local inventors. Have a Rube Goldberg or Gyro Gearloose contest for children and/or adults – they submit drawings or 3-D models. Have an Invent the Perfect Library contest, which could be in the form of a suggestion box.

5 Mother-in-Law Day first celebrated, Amarillo, TX, 1934. Have your own celebration; no jokes allowed.

7 Luther Burbank born, 1849. Botany; agriculture improvements; farming tools – their history; start a seeds-to-share collection for spring planting events; feature talk on horticulture or plant hybridization by local garden club members. Start a Flowers in the Library program.

Women's History Week. Hold a women's book discussion group one night; have 5 or 6 short lunchtime talks on women in arts, politics, history, science, medicine, sports, with speakers representing those areas.

9 Yuri Gagarin, world's first man in space, born, 1934. Coincidentally, when Gagarin was only 27, the Russians launched the first canine space traveller, March 9, 1961. (Gagarin went into space on April 12, 1961.) Hold forum on using space to attain world peace and understanding (boy, do we need it now). Let children design pet spacesuits. Start a booklist of space travel.

10 Harriet Tubman Day, who died this day, 1913. Abolition, Underground Railroad history.

11 Johnny Appleseed Day. Do a very simple display with a large old aluminum or tin saucepan, unloved enough so that you can drive a nail through bottom to spike an apple, with books on early American heroes, botanists, new medical research, recipe books. Or choose a very large apple and perch on its head a miniature saucepan. Wood from green grocer boxes good for floor and back of case.

14 Albert Einstein born, 1879. Hold a "What Hath Albert Wrought?" seminar — to give simple laymen's explanations of difficult physics concepts. (The January, 1984, *Science 84* has a great time-perception article.)

14 America's first bird sanctuary created at Pelican Island, FL, 1903. Endangered birds; winter care for birds plus year-round protection; bird call demonstration; Audubon Society/Library joint film programming.

16 National Library Week celebrated the first time, 1958. Do a display of your library's memorabilia, and ask folks to contribute snapshots and short anecdotes of the library's past.

19 Swallows will probably return to Capistrano today. Have a "Welcome all Swallows — Return to the Library" day. Why do you think many people come to the library each day? Because it feels like home. Encourage that feeling. Consider your lighting, for example. Lots of horrible fluorescent fixtures? Glare? Try warmer tones, incandescents.

20 Vernal Equinox. Sign up spring-planting teams for the grounds; start a local men's and women's gardening club or a children's gardening club. Frame your front entrance with a huge trellis of green cloth leaves, or paint Liquitex® acrylic paint leaves on the front doors, temporary of course.

National Wildlife Week. Conservation of natural resources and wildlife; history of national parks; sponsor a talk by local vet on the problem of injured or orphaned wild animals.

23 Patrick Henry said "Give me liberty, or give me death," 1775. Sponsor a debate on this subject, expand to "Better dead than red," which is possibly the modern equivalent.

23 Cookbook author Fannie Farmer born, 1857. New or old general cookbooks; specialized cookbooks with a theme — spring and fresh new ways to prepare food, including vegetables; display on controversy over salt, sugar, artificial sweeteners. Costume a balloon "fatty" and day by day the balloon would lose air, and fat.

24 Harry Houdini, magician, born, 1874. Have a "Magic of Learning" exhibit. Hire a local magician to do tricks related to books — maybe on the downtown mall.

25 Joseph Coxey led a protest army of the unemployed to Washington, where they set up a tent city near the White House, 1894. Library job services and counseling; lists of local training facilities; publicize outreach programs; set up storyhours at shelters for the homeless.

26 Nathaniel Bowditch, American mathematician, born, 1773. Display Martin Gardner's puzzle pages from *Scientific American*, perhaps with 5¢ photocopies to work the puzzles out. A lesson in New Math; one on computers and math.

30 Doctors Day — celebrated on the anniversary of the first use of ether, 1842. Assemble biographies of famous medical people; have a blood pressure clinic all day; do a display with handouts of all local medical-related information resources. Start a Friday night series of health seminars, or health care seminars.

Mardi Gras, Easter, Passover. All moveable feasts. Sponsor interfaith seminar to explain and compare Easter and Passover. Baby rabbit and chicken displays may be awfully cute, but they give people the wrong idea — that these creatures are pets to buy without thinking. On Mardi Gras, hold a mask-making day for everyone. Collects stiff paper, scissors, felt pens, felt, crepe paper, yarn, foil, colored stickers; or do found-object masks. Start saving useful materials the beginning of February: molded plastic packing for TVs and appliances; black rubber inner tubes from trucks, well washed; variety of plastic jugs; bubble pack and other interesting foam packing or carpet pads; purplish or green fruit box dividers made of pressed paper; sycamore bark, huge dead leaves, twigs; brown paper bags. End the day of mask-making with a parade with make-do drums — from Quaker Oats boxes to tin pans. Drive the demons out for a half hour — alert serious patrons a week in advance.

April

1 A Fool for the Library. Jester caps, jokes, air of gaiety and fun.
2 Hans Christian Andersen born, 1805. Celebrated as International Children's Book Day. Day-long readings of children's books, by volunteers; one special reading for which children have made colored and cut-out paper representations of characters and objects in the story — attached to sticks, like primitive puppets. Have a children's chorus sing on the steps. Some materials available from Children's Book Council, 67 Irving Place, NYC, NY 10003. If your town has one or more children's book authors (make sure their books are in the collection), invite a reading. Have a panel discussion of writers and teachers on the special needs for children's books. Sponsor an outreach program to bring a book into every poor home — as in Reading is FUNdamental program. Let everyone make a Dr. Seuss fantastical chapeau, for a reading of *The 400 Hats of Bartholomew Cubbins*.
4 Winston Smith, in George Orwell's *1984*, began his diary. If you have a library bookshop, be sure to stock diaries and blank books. Invite local stationery stores to come in and sell — share some percentage of profits. Display a wide variety of published diaries in collection. Sponsor forum on rewritten history — how it even happens today, when facts are smudged and misremembered and misreported.
5 Booker T. Washington born, 1856. Display his *Up from Slavery* autobiography; sponsor forum of local NAACP or the United Negro College Fund. Print listings of black colleges (Washington organized Tuskegee Institute in Alabama); hold a drawing to give away a children's biography of Washington.
7 World Health Day. The World Health Organization organized, 1948. If you didn't do something on Doctors Day, have a film showing of recent documentaries on worldwide drought and starvation, or on efforts to train peasant paramedics in China, South America and elsewhere. Do display on specific local health problems — pollution, high cancer rate, etc.
10 U.S. Patent Office established, 1790. Inventor Walter Hunt granted safety pin patent, 1849. Display a variety of common objects that we

take for granted — pencil, eggbeater, zipper, safety pin, tin can, light bulb, phonograph record, etc. Many fascinating books on invention and inventors.

11 Barbershop Quartet Day. The Society for the Preservation and Encouragement of Barber Shop Quartet Singing founded, 1938. Have a songfest, or start a quartet in the library — adapt an old standard with library lovin' words.

14 Noah Webster's *Dictionary* published, 1828. Display variety of dictionaries or give out booklist, and put them all together — the big dictionaries, the specialized ones for engineers or yachtsmen. Start a Fictionary Game Club, with teams to challenge each other. One person is Dictionary, and searches a large one for an unusual word. All 6 or 7 others, when asked, must tell if they know the word. If not, each player writes a short, dictionary-like definition on a slip of paper — all written the same direction, and very neatly. The Dictionary takes all the slips, adds the one written out with the real, but shortened, definition, and reads them all out clearly and straight-faced. After the reading, a 2nd may be requested. Finally, each definition is voted on. Each person who either guesses the correct definition or whose own definition is given a vote, gets a point. From a recent game played by the author and family and friends: *Haplodent*: *A toothy mammal resembling an elephant, now extinct. *That which, by happenstance or luck, is available when needed. *The metal cap on a wooden pediment. *Having molar teeth without tubercles. *A term applying to dental surgery. *A happy orthodontist. *The enzyme responsible for meiotic cell division. *The sterile offspring of a lizard and an amphibious West African frog.

16 Charlie Chaplin born, 1889. Film showings. A Little Tramp Lookalike Contest. Display of film comics, with photostatic blowups of illustrations. Movie memorabilia display — a loan exhibit. One of your library's constant aims should be to bring together artifacts and sources of facts, people with special knowledge and the place where more can be learned. Design a flyer and posters to put up all over town to help you identify people with special collections and knowledge.

23 First motion picture show in public, 1896. Have a movie shorts night; invite people to a Charlie Chaplin Charades party; send out mailing to local organizations and schools to tell them about your five new films and outlining borrowing and viewing rules.

24 Library of Congress established, 1800. Do a bulletin board about the purpose of LC, and how your own library is there to serve its community. Organize a letter-writing campaign to your state or national representatives, emphasizing need for continued funds and fond attention. It is an outrage for library funds to be eliminated in Federal budgets.

25 First auto license plates issued, by NY State, 1901. April is also National Automobile Month. How about a special book display in local auto showrooms; borrow fancy and interesting accessories or parts for a display; have a car interior decoration contest; if there's a local collector, see if there's a small runabout or other car that could be driven right into the library for display. Do a special bookmobile campaign.

26 Frederick Law Olmsted, celebrated landscape architect whose works include NY's Central Park, born, 1822. Sponsor a guided tour of a local park, to acquaint people with the designed features. Begin a library landscaping improvement program; start a fund for a reading gazebo — outdoors or inside.

May

1 May Day and Law Day. In Hawaii it's Lei Day. Flower baskets made up with plastic flowers and books, all over the library (or real flowers if you can get them loaned). Libraries and the Law — from censoring, to revelation of borrowers' choices, to setting up gifts in wills, to overdue books.

1 The first U.S. postal card issued by government, 1873. Display postcards depicting flowers or animals or judges and policemen. (Most deltiologists — postcard collectors — love a chance to show off their collections.) Have a supply of 14¢ (or is it 15¢ now?) postals, to sell at cost, plus crayons, pens, rubber stamps for decorating them. Let everyone who comes in May 1 make a postcard — perhaps to go out and send to the library for a special display the end of May.

3 Friends of Animals, a humanitarian organization, founded, 1957. Caring for animals is a good way to encourage caring for all of life. Some excellent books on animals' relationship to humans are: Diolé, Philippe, *The Errant Ark: Man's Relationship with Animals*. NYC: Putnam's, 1974; Ruesch, Hans. *Slaughter of the Innocent*. NYC: Bantam, 1978; Singer, Peter, *Animal Liberation: A New Ethics for Our Treatment of Animals*. NYC: Avon, 1975; Turner, E.S., *All Heaven in a Rage*. NYC: St. Martin's, 1965. As Diolé put it: "It is time for a new contract between man and animal."

5 Christopher Morley born, 1890. Do a Haunted Bookshop display in a big case, or a corner of a room, with a sheet-covered ghost and mystery books. Collect as many mystery books as donations and discards as you can find and sell at desk. Do special bookmobile event, and rename your vehicle "Parnassus on Wheels" for the week.

Be Kind to Animals Week begins around now. See May 3. Also: A division of The Humane Society of the U.S., The National Association for the Advancement of Humane Education, publishes a wide and important number of materials, including *Kind News,* a quarterly tabloid for young people; also a magazine, *Humane Education,* for educators (and librarians?); plus curriculum guides at 4 levels to reach children from preschool through grade 6—but the concepts are useful with adults. NAAHE has teaching materials catalog, with booklets, filmstrips and films. Write The Norma Terris Humane Education Center, POB 362, E. Haddam, CT 06423.

8 The De Soto expedition reached banks of the Mississippi, 1541. Have a River Discovery Day, or Creek or Spring Discovery Day. Readings about freshwater biology, river industries, pollution of water. Create a scrapbook for Local History Div. from the trek—photographs of the river, boating, riverside business and beautification, etc. Have everyone take notes or contribute a poem or aphorism or observation. This kind of local history research and exploration can be applied to many aspects of community life, and is a good way to get media attention, and encourage participation from all kinds of people who will then feel a stronger bond with the library.

9 Berlin was the site of the first Nazi book burning, 1930. Display on dangers of censorship based on any kind of ideology. Display *Fahrenheit 451.*

11 Johnny Appleseed (John Chapman) born, 1768. See March 11. Do promotion with local orchard on planting apple trees — perhaps you can get nursery to donate small trees, or sell to card-carrying library users at special discount. Have apple pie bakeoff and fundraiser. Borrow antique apple parers, corers and slicers to do display on kitchen collectibles.

12 Edward Lear, English author and illustrator famed for his limericks, born, 1812. Have a Limericking Day—pick a theme: libraries, spring, some issue of topical interest. Display large blow-ups of Lear's fabulous drawings.

15 Frank Baum, creator of the Oz stories, born, 1856. Have a scarecrow contest, with real scarecrows created in regiments on the lawn. Do a tornado display. Did you know Kansas has the lowest expected wind speed of any state? Only 9 miles an hour!

16 America's first 5¢ piece authorized, 1866. Have a one-day "Reader, can you spare a nickel?" campaign. Have a large facsimile—photostatic or drawn on foil—of a buffalo nickel and suspend over contribution jars. Specify a goal. Or make a one-week-only "All Book Fines 5¢" offer to get back overdue books.

16 The impeachment of President Andrew Johnson failed by 1 vote, 1868. Do bulletin board on impeachment attempts of the past, on grounds for impeachment according to the Constitution.

17 Racial segregation in schools declared unconstitutional by Supreme Court, 1954. Have a staff meeting with volunteers and representatives from community to discuss ways to improve outreach programs to minorities.

20 Charles Lindbergh flew Atlantic in 1922, landing in Paris; 5 years later Amelia Earhart made the first solo woman's flight over same approximate course. Have an Aviation Buff day. See if you can get a local skywriter to add "VISIT THE LIBRARY" to his message. See if it's possible to set up a temporary heliport near the library for a bird's-eye view of it and the city with paid helicopter rides. Start a "Look Up!" campaign for raising money.

21 Fats Waller born, 1904. Have an "Ain't Misbehavin'" concert in the late afternoon or evening, encourage high-steppin' and fancy dress.

24 Brooklyn Bridge opened, 1883. Display bridge books, such as David McCullough's on the B.B. Invite local engineer to give talk on bridge design, or hold an open forum on a controversial local bridge — to widen or not, or the need and funding for nationwide bridge maintenance. Have someone from Traffic Department talk about safe driving on bridges in all conditions. Start a "Bridge to the Future" fund for the oral history department. Publicize an outreach program.

25 Ralph Waldo Emerson, philosopher/author, born, 1803. One famous essay is *Friendship*. Have a Day of Friendship at library — have people bring a friend who've never been to your branch; sign up members for a Friends group; encourage children to make a new friend at the library, or read aloud to a friend, or write a poem or song on friendship, or do a research paper on friendship, or sign a Library Pal Pact with a school friend to come to the library and read a certain number of books during the summer.

25 Babe Ruth hit his 714th, and last, home run, 1935. Take the bookmobile out to the ballpark and serve popcorn and crackerjacks, with tissues to clean hands. Sponsor a library team — announce the first practice session for a June 12th game.

27 Amelia Bloomer, famed for her sporty bloomers, born 1818. Have a fashion show with most controversial fashions available in town, or historical costume display. Have a fashion-forecast design contest all day, open to everyone. Predict fashion look a year from today. Have a bicycle race with bloomers the costume. Have a Bloomer Garden Party.

30 The first U.S. daily paper, the *Pennsylvania Evening Post*, published, 1783. Make a poster of President Eisenhower's proclamation of National Newspaper Week in 1958: "A strong society of free men must be kept fully informed. Liberty can flourish only in the climate of truth."

June

Dairy Month. If your town has milk delivery persons on routes, perhaps they'll carry a PR notice for you: "Good morning! Wouldn't it be nice to have a book to read with milk and cookies? Visit your library." Do display on osteoporosis and the need for supplemental calcium in women's diets, with a talk by a doctor.

2 Johnny Weissmuller — Tarzan, the "noble savage" — born, 1904. Ask gymnasts for local Y to perform on their mats in front of the library. Hang vines over entrance with sign: "Jungle Full of Wild Ideas, Just Inside" or show film on chimpanzee or gorilla research.

5 Spanish writer Federico García Lorca born in Spain, 1889. Have an Hispanic Culture week, with readings in two languages. Greet everyone who enters with Buenos días, señor, señora, señorita!

5 World Environment Day. First UN Conference on the Human Environment opened, 1972. What is the most pressing environmental need or problem in your community? Give space to a display by qualified local groups. If there's a debate going on — in the editorial pages of the newspaper, for example — hold a formal one. If you think your community doesn't have a problem, think about acid rain, nuclear waste, industrial pollution. Have a photographic display of deterioriation of carved monuments or stone trim on buildings. Take acid readings for a month of local standing water body.

7 Paul Gauguin, the French painter who lived in the Marquesas Islands to paint, born, 1848. Show island films; feature island books — from vacation spots to Robinson Crusoe. If your town has an island, have a fundraising picnic. Lobby to name a traffic island in your community for the library: "Stop, Look, Listen & Think: Library Island."

7 The TV show "$64,000 Question" aired first, 1955. Have a trivia quiz show, perhaps sponsored by radio station or cable TV in your area, with school children. Fund raiser for 64¢, $64, $640.

8 Ice cream first advertised, 1786. See if local ice cream franchise like "Mister Softee" or "Carvel" or other will name a flavor especially for you, just for the day or week. Will they give you a popular flavor? How about "Liberry Ripple, Booklet Chip, Vanillibrary, or Favorite Author. See if they'll set up a cone booth in front of library and contribute 10¢ for each cone.

12 Baseball invented by Abner Doubleday at Cooperstown, NY, 1839. Time for your first game.

12 Children's Day. Plan picnic with story-telling, perhaps as part of a community-wide program of events. Give out special bookmarks to children. Set up a story-telling nook at playgrounds.

14 Margaret Bourke-White born, 1906. Sponsor a photo contest with local

camera clubs; hold a class on journalistic photography for teenagers; invite people to take pictures in and around the library all morning, with proper releases signed by anyone appearing in picture, for a display 2 weeks later. Write Polaroid Corporation about their program to place cameras in libraries: 549 Technology Square, Cambridge, MA 02139.

15 Benjamin Franklin flew his kite and key during an electrical storm, 1752. Have post cards or envelopes printed up with a representation of Ben, Kite and Key and the legend: "The key to an electric personality: Suchandsuch Library." Give out kite-shaped bookmarks printed with a key and the library hours at public parks, malls.

15 Celluloid, an ivory substitute made first into billiard balls, patented, 1869. Have a pool tournament with borrowed tables in main hall, all proceeds to go to library. Display everyday and decorative things of plastic, celluloid or Bakelite, borrowed from Friends, staffers, etc.

16 The Alaska Gold Rush began in 1897. Do an exhibit in conjunction with local travel agencies on gold-panning vacations available in the Northwest, Virginia and South America.

Father's Day. The Friday before, have a special program to help children select books to take home to read aloud to their fathers. Have a father and child story-telling. Have a group discussion led by fathers who have opted to be house-husbands. Start a single parents book-discussion group.

21 Summer Solstice begins about now. Have a night's summer festival, play "Summertime," show *Summer and Smoke*. Have a "Cool Summer Drink" recipe contest ... results to be published shortly after to raise money.

22 Anne Morrow Lindbergh born, 1906. Do a special display of her *Gift from the Sea*. The best self-help book ever. Seashell display with books on the shore, on the sea.

23 William Sholes patented his typewriter, 1868. Throw a speed-typing exhibition or contest; offer to type a portrait in the lobby — for contributions; borrow the most peculiar and interesting specimens from local typewriter repair shop for a display called QWERTY. If you have a word processor, demonstrate that.

24 Flying saucers reported near Mount Rainier, 1947. Offer a talk, a film, books on space. Sponsor a contest for children to design a space ship after a description in a book, to make up a sentence of space traveler words, draw a space suit, make an outer space inhabitant's mask. Have a Frisbee game.

Full Moon. Have a howling contest on the lawn, after the moon is out. Go on a moon treasure hunt, using books in the library.

25 George Orwell, satirist and social soothsayer, born, 1903. Cull examples of contemporary Newspeak; have students compile a dictionary of opposites. Kick off a voter registration drive, or do up a booklist of readings on voting and the history of voter's rights. Read parts of 1984 or Animal Farm over a hidden loudspeaker — spooky as you can — and invite people to an Orwellian evening.

27 Helen Keller born, 1880. Show film on Keller. Demonstrate ASL. Publicize your outreach programs for the blind, deaf and physically disadvantaged. Do a demo of "hearing" by vibrations. I learned at a disco recently, where admittedly the sound is horribly loud, that by holding one of the many balloons floating around against my chest, and by standing very near a speaker, the vibrations of the music are transmitted in a most extraordinary way.

July

2 Lawrence Welk's first show on TV, 1955. Have a dance — waltzes, polkas and rhumba. "It's wunnerful, wunnerful" — the book collection on music, dancing, early TV at the library.

4 Independence Day. Have children, or new citizens, or a group of older people, write statements on freedom, and what it means to them. Hand out Firecracker Safety Tips. Cooperate with local civic group having a fireworks display, and publicize one of the bursts as representing "Intellectual Freedom."

6 Beatrix Potter, creator of Peter Rabbit, born, 1866. Start a Peter Rabbit Endowment (or Peter Rabbit Chair) for books on pets and animal care for children. Have readings.

6 Arthur Godfrey's *Talent Scouts* TV show first aired in 1948. Hold a talent show, with every act somehow related to books, information-seeking, the library, intellectual freedom. If you've never seen someone in a book costume tap-dancing, you've got a treat in store.

7 A great day for jazz in 1937. Louis Armstrong recorded his "Alexander's Ragtime Band," and Count Basie recorded "One o'Clock Jump." Have a noontime jazz-recording concert. Sponsor a jazz discussion, or sponsor a local jazz band to perform at the very end of the day — trade their performance for the sure publicity. Ask members of a jazz record collectors' station in on this — with PSAs and bits of jazz.

9 National Fast Day inaugurated, 1832. Ask people to give a meal's money to a charity aiding Africa; the dessert money to the library. OXFAM America, 115 Broadway, Boston, MA 02116.

10 James McNeill Whistler born, 1834. Have a "Bring Your Mom and Set a Spell" Day. Can you borrow an assortment of homey chairs, particularly rocking chairs, to group or scatter in various parts of the library? Add coffee and tea, footstools. Make it an annual event.

12 Henry David Thoreau born, 1817. If your community has a pond, sponsor a nature walk, with a pre-walk conservation film. Or have a four-leaf clover search on the library lawn; a birdwatch; a plant inventory on library property. Have a Thoreau reading. Do books on pond life, dowsing, seclusion, whittling, pedestrianism, beards, walking tours, log cabin building, forest life.

12 George Eastman, photographic pioneer, born, 1854. Announce a Photo-Discovery Drive to form an archive of photographs showing the library, and surrounding neighborhood. Call a meeting with the local historical society about developing a collection of photographs of local people reading.

14 First Esperanto book published, 1887. If there's an Esperanto society chapter in your community, sponsor a talk or a simple language lesson.

14 Woodie Guthrie born, 1912. Have folksinging, folk stories, hog-calling contest right in the library — shake the dust off the books for another year. Feature Foxfire books, oral history-taking, crafts. Display your Folkways recordings, and play some.

16 Roald Amundsen, Norwegian explorer and South Pole discoverer, born, 1872. Films, books on pole exploration.

17 The oldest humorous periodical, *Punch*, began publishing in London, 1841. Have a Punch and Judy puppet show or an Italian Pulcinella show. Offer selection of contemporary humor magazines such as *National Lampoon*. Sponsor a "write a caption" contest, or start an evening series reading humorists such as Thurber, Perelman, Wodehouse, Bombeck. Show Monty Python tapes.

20 Astronauts Neil Armstrong and Buzz (Edwin) Aldrin, Jr., walked on moon, 1969. Have a moonrise astronomy lesson. Display comic books on space stories from the '50s. Have a cheese day, or see if a local photographer would like to set up a crescent moon prop for photographing people, the old-fashioned way.

21 National Women's Hall of Fame dedicated in 1979. Do a display, plus a series of talks, of local women — including the unsung heroines who get things done, the people in private life whose lives still touch others.

24 Amelia Earhart, aviator who flew the Atlantic five years after Lindbergh, born, 1898. Offer a sheet of clue words for people to learn how to research, and how to follow up leads they come across by accident. Simple key words like air travel, ballooning, pilots to start. Then use Poole's Index of 19th Century periodical literature to show how far back people have written about air travel. Do up list of mysterious or total disappearances.

26 America's postal system established, 1775. Set up a letter-writing area, try it as a permanent thing, with two study carrels and a few books of poetry, Bartlett's, collected letters.

27 U.S. State Department created by Congress, 1789. Diplomacy, world history, the relationship between the UN and US foreign policy.

29 Author Booth Tarkington born, 1869. Feature books such as his *Alice Adams* or *Penrod* with display on artifacts of growing up 100 years ago.

August

1 Herman Melville born, 1819. Display on natural history of whales; whales as endangered species; Greenpeace; cetaceans in general, including the studies with "talking" dolphins.

2 The first mailboxes in America were set up, in Boston, 1858. Have a letter campaign to state and federal organizations or representatives about library support. Come up with a new motto for your postage meter to print. Sell I Love Libraries postal cards.

3 Harvard beat Yale in first intercollegiate rowing race, 1853. You mightn't have sculls, but a rowboat or canoe race could be held with a library team. Sponsor water safety program; push water sports books and magazines; show a film on boating — one little-seen film, very heartwarming, is National Film Board of Canada's *Steady as She Goes*, on building a ship in a bottle.

4 The Chautauqua Literary & Scientific Circle founded, 1874. Inaugurate an evening Chautauqua series — it'd be great in a large tent — with lectures and films on varied subjects. Serve lemonade and biscuits. At least for the opening event, borrow a large auctioneer's tent, or get a party tent rented and paid for as a contribution.

7 Ralph Bunche, United Nations diplomat and statesman, born, 1904. Have a world peace program, or one on brotherhood of all people, with churches, ethical societies, social agencies participating.

8 Charles Bulfinch, probably America's first professional architect, born, 1763. Mount exhibit of architectural drawings for branch libraries; have contest for school children to design a library of future. Sponsor a walking tour of downtown, with information sheet on scope of your local history architectural files. NYPL has a great collection of 19th and early 20th century photographs, filed street by street, avenue by avenue.

8 Newspaperman Charles A. Dana, born 1819. Get out all the newspapers you subscribe to and put them up front for a day or week. Invite local newspaper people and journalism students to come on a private tour of stacks, with explanation of wide variety of useful materials library has for them.

9 The Father of Angling, Izaak Walton, born, 1593. Sponsor a series on fishing — with a film, a demonstration of fly-tying, a display of special flies, readings from Walton's *The Compleat Angler*, conservation plans for local parks. Fish shaped bookmarks — "Don't Be the One That Got Away" — can be distributed, with an abbreviated bibliography, or schedule for lecture/film series. Have a discussion group to delve into Hemingway's "The Old Man and the Sea."

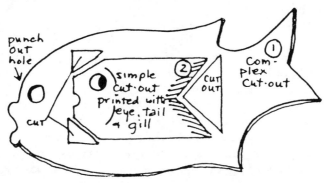

9 Have a moment of silence for the victims of the Nagasaki atomic bombing. Since then, we have all become victims of the bomb, all hostages to it.

10 The Smithsonian Institution (the "Nation's Attic") founded, 1846. Sponsor a Discovery Day like auction houses do. Borrow a natural history expert, a geologist, and a couple of antiques/collectibles experts. Let people carry in objects for ID. And be ready to point out books and other materials on same subjects. Display your own attic artifacts — relative to your library's history or local history.

11 Gifford Pinchot, America's first professional forester and conservationist, born, 1865. You might lead a Terrific Tree Tour of the community, pointing out notable specimens — the largest cherry, the strangest sycamore, the shortest and fattest apple, the birch or dogwood with the most branches at the bottom. Do a local history display on a local historical tree. Have a "Tree 'n' Me" photo contest, or a Best Tree for Reading expedition. Or have a nature poetry reading out under the trees. Or make a story-telling papier-mâché tree for the children's room.

12 Film director Cecil B. De Mille born, 1881. And on the 13th, in 1899, Alfred Hitchcock was born. Have a movie festival, a movie trivia contest, start a video or Super-8 movie-making program for a later showing of 3 minute films, made in and around the library.

12 George Wesley Bellows, painter, born, 1882. Some of his vitality comes from his subjects, which include people doing sports. Do a sport-in-art display including sports photos from the local newspaper's morgue. Because of the animation and coordination of athletes, often sports photos are among the most aesthetically pleasing news photos.

13 William Caxton, first English printer, born, c.1422. Put up "Who Is Caxton?" posters — inviting people to come to the library for the answer.

If there's a real life Caxton in your community, perhaps he would like to participate in the festivities, and help people sign up for library cards. Use Caxton's Day as an excuse to send a band of library angels out into the street with a provocative flyer about the great discoveries to be made at the library.

14 John Galsworthy, English novelist, born, 1867. Start a "Foresight Saga" for your community or future library plans. Conduct a survey, not confined to library card-holders, with a town meeting at the library, or on the mall, or in the school auditorium.

15 Sir Walter Scott, Scottish poet/novelist, born, 1771. I bet you didn't know Scott wrote at least one cookbook review — in the July, 1805, *Edinburgh Review*. Do a Romance in the Kitchen series, with the idea of cookbooks as literature. M.F.K. Fisher's works are prime examples. Reprint a recipe, with a modern how-to, from oldest cookbook in your collection. Or compile a list to hand out of Scottish vocabulary words (about 2 hours with a good etymological dictionary will give you a huge supply) that people would enjoy tossing into their conversations. Wouldn't you love to come upon a break-dancing teen using words like "ken" and "nicht" and "auld"?

17 David Crockett, frontiersman, born, 1786. Have a New Frontiers booklist prepared — robotics, gene splicing, space exploration, or push the idea that knowledge, by its very nature, is a constantly expanding new frontier. (See next two items.)

17 The first successful trans-Atlantic balloon flight, 1978.

18 Meriwether Lewis, explorer, born, 1774. Have a Pushing the Frontiers Week, celebrating exploration and expedition. Add space, undersea, arctic adventures.

19 Seth Thomas, pioneer clockmaker from Connecticut, born, 1785. Have an Old Clock Clinic, with a local clock repairer to demonstrate something like pendulum setting. Do up a Timely Tips checklist, for using the library. Let children make their own hourglasses, using 2 Pyrex funnels, masking tape, and cardboard to seal top and bottom. Let them experiment with different kinds of fillers — sand, eggshells (baked and crushed with rolling pin or mortar and pestle), celery seeds, birdseed, beebees.

19 John Cotton Dana, great librarian and museum director, with a very original mind, born, 1865. Most people don't even know what the library director looks like, so have a "Meet the Director" Day. Or get all the head librarians in town — corporations, schools, colleges — to come to a luncheon to discuss ways of sharing publicity and building readership.

21 The Lincoln-Douglas debates began, 1858. Those weren't the only famous political debates. Is there a local contest for a congressional seat? An upcoming city council vacancy? Or what about spokespersons for local Democratic and Republican clubs debating an issue such as Freedom of Information, or public funds for libraries.

24 The National Library was burned, along with the White House, by British captors of Washington, DC, 1814. Thomas Jefferson sold his books to the government to start again; it became LC. Start a Save-A-Book campaign. Let people adopt a book that needs repair, or replace it. Or one that needs rebinding or microfilming. Or let them contribute to a general fund for such work. Do up a list for a good nucleus library to send off to college with students — don't use standard selections, use your imagination.

25 The National Park Service was established, 1916. Hold a forum on public lands in your area, and their proper care and use. Sponsor a day trip by bus to nearby national park. Do a cleanup-and-picnic at your local civic park, with a booklist from the library.

26 Frans Hals, great Dutch portraitist, born, 1584. His vivacious portraits are so attractive today that we can easily fall in love with his subjects. Have a day of portrait photography posed in the library — either a prepared set, or in a favorite nook. Maybe one photographer a day for a week, with the library to get some part of the proceeds.

28 Leo Tolstoi, great Russian essayist and novelist, born, 1828. He was also noted as a social reformer of the best kind. Share the likenesses of the Russian people and Americans by fostering appreciation of Russian literature.

28 The first American speeding ticket issued in Newport, RI, 1904. If there's a MADD (Mothers Against Drunk Driving) chapter, hold a meeting at the library. Use government serials to explain case for 55mph law.

29 John Locke, English philosopher who influenced our Founding Fathers, born, 1632. His *An Essay Concerning Human Understanding* is worth browsing now. Especially Chap. XIX, "Of Enthusiasm." Some great lines for libraries.

29 Author Oliver Wendell Holmes born, 1809. Have a "Breakfast Table" get-together for local business people to acquaint them with library services. Or a morale-boosting staff breakfast.

September

1 Bobby Fischer became America's first modern-era world chess champion, 1972. Open a chess tourney; set up a game-borrowing, or a partner-borrowing program. Have a Knights of the Roundtable discussion group — women and men.

4 Richard Rogers Bowker born, 1848. What would librarians do without RR? Time to have a library party, just for yourselves.

6 Hiroshigi, famed Japanese printmaker, died, 1858. Japanese art is due for a renaissance of interest, to match the interest in Japanese fashion and food. Have a Japanese Culture Week, help form an Asian Society to foster all Oriental arts.

7 Grandma Moses, America's most famous folk artist, born, 1860. Have an art show co-sponsored with local retirement homes. Get elder citizens and children together for a day of painting and drawing — perhaps to pair up for future excursions. Broaden to a "That's How It Was" series, where elders can show and tell youngsters how they did things.

Banned Books Week begins about now. Do a small display explaining your library's position on controversial books and access to them. Also on your formal procedures for handling public complaints about particular books or classes of printed matter, and about the library's rules for acceptance of materials.

10 Elias Howe's sewing machine patented, 1846. Put up exhibit of sewing books; have a sewing machine rep or salesperson set up in the crafts department or front lobby and sew a library banner — complete with motto, logo, fringe and rick-rack trim. Or announce a library department banner contest; contestants choose a category.

Grandparents Day. This is the 2nd Sunday in the month. Sponsor a grandparent/grandchild read-in on the Saturday or Monday. Have "adoptable" grandfolks on hand for children whose grandparents live far away.

15 James Fenimore Cooper born, 1789. Another reason to call it a Frontier Year. (See August 17.)

15 Agatha Christie born, 1890. Do a display or booklist of mysteries that take place in the library.

17 The United States Constitution signed, 1787. This is Citizenship Day. Invite new citizens, particulary recently naturalized or registered alien citizens to a special Multinational Day to introduce to library services.

18 Samual Johnson, storied lexicographer and author, born, 1709. He did everything, including writing essays, plays, a dictionary, and novels, and was the most sparkling example of a "literary drudge" ever produced. In his honor, start a Literary Club, for book discussions, creative writing, creating a local slang or usage dictionary.

19 Arthur Rackham, illustrator of many books, especially children's, born, 1867. In honor of his last, and possibly best, work — build a model Toad Hall of papier-mâché, using Rackham's illustration. Let children design their own, or create masks of all the characters. Have a tour of a local pond or stream, or plant a willow.

Autumnal Equinox. Collect freshly-fallen leaves to press between waxed paper until perfectly dry. Use to create collages, or for a traditional

Japanese form of decoupage, by glueing leaves to small boxes or flat picture frames, then varnishing. Have a Biggest Pumpkin Contest.

20 Novelist Upton Sinclair born, 1878. Most famed now as a muckraker who effected change in several aspects of life, he wrote over 80 books. *Oil!* from 1927, *World's End*, 1940, and *The Goose-Step* of 1923 – which deals with the effect of capitalism on institutions of learning. Interesting to hold a seminar on how far into the future, and how clearly, some writers seemed to peer. Do a discussion panel with local investigative reporters and lawyers on how muckraking works in a democracy.

21 H(erbert) G(eorge) Wells born, 1866. Sponsor an "experiment in autobiography" (as per his book) for children or adolescents. Suggest they use one sheet of paper and combine words and small drawings to tell their story. Later make a hall display. Or do a Time Machine art show, with children depicting one thing they'd expect to see if they traveled far forward or far back in time. Hand out booklist of time travel stories. NYPL did one entitled "Amazing Journeys Through Time and Space" that included time voyages such as Jack Finney's *Time and Again*, Mark Twain's *A Connecticut Yankee in King Arthur's Court*, and Arthur Conan Doyle's *The Lost World* (which reminded me of a Ray Bradbury story). *Timescape*, by Gregory Benford, is an important contemporary novel about nebulous time; *Time's Arrows*, by Richard Morris, is a fascinating new book on the vagaries of time.

22 Physicist/chemist Michael Faraday born, 1755. Noted for electrical experiments. Find out if someone in your community – school, college, plant laboratory – could do a live demonstration of a chemical, electrical or physical experiment, in the library. Many patrons will not have seen a chemical experiment in many decades. Do a booklist of various grades of lab science books, and biographies. Do a display of our country's electrical pioneers – Franklin, Edison, Tesla. Set up a demonstration of how electricity affects us every day with a team: one turns on a lamp, the other lights a candle; one beats an egg with a fork, another with a mixer; one sharpens a pencil with a knife, the other with electricity; one sweeps, one vacuums.

23 William McGuffey born, 1800. Schools, educational standards, ERIC (Educational Resources Information Center), the three "R"s, mnemonic learning, school and curriculum design, teaching as a profession – all subjects for discussion or display.

24 F. Scott Fitzgerald, born, 1896. The Twenties; disillusioned youth – a longtime phenomenon; jazz, Art Deco design.

26 George Gershwin born, 1898. Roll in the piano, and play the blues. Write a Library Blues contest. Sell sheet music. Have a Rhapsody in Blue day, with Gershwin recordings at a lunch concert, with blue crepe paper streamers, have everyone invited to wear blue – staff and public. Serve blueberry muffins, or sell them.

27 Cartoonist/caricaturist Thomas Nast born, 1840. Honor political car-
toonists in general by selecting one or more interesting old ones from
a book or collected political cartoons (such as J.C. Suarez's book), and
make clear photocopies without captions. Let people write captions.
Also on the 27th, in 1792, the great English illustrator/cartoonist
George Cruikshank was born. Build a display around works of both
men, or invite local political cartoonist(s) to do a demonstration.

28 Kate Douglas Wiggin born, 1856. Noted for *Rebecca of Sunnybrook
Farm*, and poetry anthologies. Have a costumed reading of *Rebecca*; let
children create wall mural of the farm. Start a children's poetry
reading/writing group in cooperation with schools.

30 St. Jerome's Feast Day. Patron saint of scholars and librarians (and
reportedly anti-women, but we can forget that now). He translated the
Bible into the Latin Vulgate version. Have a staff party, for absolutely
everyone who works at the library, to strengthen bonds. Have a special
showing of a brand new film, just for the staff; introduce new services
you want to push. Make every single staff person, including those who
work at "menial" tasks, want to know more about the library. And if
you are struggling to get the great booboisie into the library, wondering
why the entire public doesn't want to tear down your doors, practice by
showing each and every employee what the library can do for them.

October

1 The great, late, black Model T Ford first marketed, 1908. If there's a
"brass and gas" club in your community, or someone who owns a
restored T, or any other ancient auto, display inside the library or in the
parking lot. Or have an oldest cars in town rally. Display car repair or
automobilia-collecting materials. Find if someone has an old T con-
verted to a tractor (as Ford sold plans to do).

2 Groucho Marx born, 1895. Humor, early TV, American humorists and
comedians, a list of nonsensical euphemisms (like horsefeathers and
hen's teeth). Have a bike horn concert. (See November 30.)

3 "Father Knows Best" first aired, 1954. Encourage children to bring their
fathers to a special reading aloud program. Ask people of all ages to
write a few lines about what they learned from their fathers.

5 Denis Diderot, French encyclopedist/letter-writter/philosopher, born,
1713. Two of his works, written when he was 36, are on the blind and
how they learn, and on the deaf and dumb. His 28-volume encyclopedia
is still a model, and the illustrations have been widely reproduced. Use
his birthday as an excuse to start raising a fund for new encyclopedias,

or a series of programs to bring sighted and blind together, to sponsor American Sign Language classes for the general public and staff. At least one police department in the US is learning ASL to better deal with deaf citizens, including miscreants.

5 The Greenpeace Foundation formed in Vancouver, BC, 1970. Frequently in the news for their humanitarian incursions into foreign waters to protest whale slaughter, etc., Greenpeace offers an example of bravery and dedication, altruism and loving-kindness. Show whale or ocean life films, etc.

6 Jenny Lind, the Swedish Nightingale operatic singer, born, 1820. Have an evening of light operatic music, art song, or popular show tunes. In 1920, a concert to commemorate Lind was held with a singer impersonating her. So successful that over 500 concerts were eventually given. Maybe you could organize, with a fine young singer, such a costumed evening.

7 James Whitcomb Riley, comic poet, born, 1849. Have a pumpkin day, with a reading of *When the Frost is on the Punkin*.

8 Eddie Rickenbacker born, 1890. Aviation, airplanes, heroes of the air, difference between air and space. Further afield: air rights, clean air.

International Letter Writing Week. The first week that includes Eleanor Roosevelt's October 11, 1884 birthday. She believed that writing letters to people in other lands fostered friendship, brotherhood and world peace. Announce a Pen Pal program. UNICEF provides children and adults with a list of agencies who then provide names of willing pen pals. Send SASE to Information Center on Children's Cultures, UNICEF, 331 E. 38th St., NYC, NY, 10016.

Flat, glass-top display cases set up in central court hold exhibits of letters from interesting people in your manuscript collection. Or, if someone in your library has collected funny or unusual or interesting mail addressed to the library over many years, display those. Or display envelopes — most libraries receive mail that is very peculiarly addressed. Offer collected letters books at checkout. Do fountain pen or advertising pencil display; history of writing instruments, antique typewriters.

15 Economist John Kenneth Galbraith born, 1908. Hold a "conspicuous consumer" day — and collect canned foods for local charity, or canned pet food for local Humane Society or SPCA.

16 Lexicographer Noah Webster born, 1758. Sponsor a Fictionary Tournament; push vocabulary building books or start such a class. (See August 15 and September 18.)

17 Albert Einstein immigrated to the US, 1933. Display some simplified scientific theories, famous immigrants, new books on old Einstein theories.

20 Mickey Mantle born, 1931. Baseball, sports injuries clinics, collecting baseball memorabilia and cards.

21 Hokusai, famed Japanese woodcut engraver, for whom no subject was too insignificant, born, 1760. Have a Day of Printmaking — woodcuts, linoleum, raw potatoes. Or do monoprints, where a picture is first done in wet gooey paint or ink on a piece of paper, then turned over and transferred with hand pressure onto a piece of absorbent paper or cloth.

22 The Metropolitan Opera in NYC opened, 1883, with performance of "Faust." Have a Faust recording concert; have a talk by local singing teacher on opera; do a display of opera books, or a display of stories on the Faustian theme.

24 United Nations Day. Stress world peace, world understanding, ethnic heritage, UNICEF. See if there can be a program for your community or library to send books to other countries.

25 Geoffrey Chaucer, early English poet, died, 1400. Have a series of your own *Canterbury Tales*, where local people, each related to one of the characters in the *Tales*, meet with staffers to discuss ideas on how to motivate people to use the library. Make them Ambassadors at Large in the community, and give them inside-dopester knowledge and familiarity with the many services offered.

29 The New York Stock Market collapsed, 1929. Announce a four-week seminar on investing. Arrange for brokers or account executives from different firms in your town to be represented — either on a panel, or as speakers at each session.

31 Halloween and National Magic Day (Harry Houdini died on this date, 1926). Mask-making and card tricks. Have a class to teach anyone who wants to learn a very simple card trick. Do display on the original religious background of All Hallows Eve.

November

1 Goldsmith/sculptor Benvenuto Cellini born, 1500. Copy out selections from his autobiography. Line a case with gold wrapping paper and display books on Italian art. (See November 19.)

1 The Rainbow Bridge over Niagara Falls opened, 1941. Let children build a fanciful bridge with colored crepe paper and construction paper from one section of children's room to another. Start a fund for a small Rainbow Bridge on library lawn — if you have a pond, spring or goldfish pond. If it's sunny, demonstrate a mini-rainbow by using very fine spritzer of water out in sun.

6 John Philip Sousa born, 1854. American band music, marches, local school bands — see if you can have a concert. Give a tuba player a chance to play in the best acoustical spot in the library.

American Education Week begins about now. (Second week in November.) Send out flyers to school teachers to emphasize your committment to and participation in the educative process. Sponsor a panel discussion for the general public at the library, or something on community involvement in education. Offer space to a continuing education group. Pin a big paper "R" on each and every staffer: "There are more than 3 Rs at the library!" Collect some of the strangest subjects covered at the library—say a whole new selection of "R"s, and have a noteworthy, photogenic event a week or so before.

8 Edmund Halley, English astronomer who is most famous for his comet, born, 1656. In 1682 he saw the great comet, and foretold its return in 1758 (it was on time).

National Children's Book Week. (See April 2.)

16 W(illiam) C(hristopher) Handy born, 1873. As "Father of the Blues," and composer of one of the best-loved compositions—"Ol' Man River"—he can be celebrated with playing of records, some live piano playing. (See September 26.)

18 First Mickey Mouse movie shown, 1928, called "Steamboat Willie." On November 14, 1765, steamboat inventor Robert Fulton was born. Make this Steamboat Week—see if you can get someone to demonstrate a model steam engine. Photocopy illustrations of various steam engines, with captions. Do an Art of Disney display including animation. Steamboats and paddleboats on the Mississippi.

19 Bertel Thorvaldsen, Danish sculptor, born, 1770. Make November Sculpture Month, with exhibits of local work, booklists, demonstrations of marble working, wood carving, armature building for plaster modeling. Start on a sculpted papier-mâché door, lintel or gateway inside the library. Low relief, perhaps with scenes from classics. Ground-up newsprint dust, available in craft shops, mixed with starch and white household glue, will produce a medium fine enough to really sculpt. Paint with colors or with gold.

Thanksgiving Day. Have a Thanksgiving Day celebration. Do up bookmarks with quotes of thinking. Say "Think you" all day. Fill a cornucopia with books, tapes and some ornamental gourds for a "Use Your Gourd" Thanksgiving Day table decoration. Have a pin-the-tail-on-the-turkey game in children's room, after children have made individual turkey tail feathers and lettered with the title of a favorite book or author.

25 Andrew Carnegie, great friend of libraries, born, 1838. Even if your library isn't a Carnegie-endowed institution, undoubtedly you've benefited. Sponsor a "Book Endowment Day": pass out flyers and put up posters—everywhere, including the library—about giving memorial books to library. If you don't have a staffer who can consult with people about possible gifts, make up a book gift list that's kept current. See about getting a special gift bookplate, the design or designs contributed by local artists or bookbinders or graphic design studio.

26 Sojourner Truth Day. The great, freed-slave abolitionist, who travelled the country giving talks to women's groups, and selling her "shadow for the substance" (her photographic likeness for food and clothing). Have special program on abolitionists, civil rights, women's rights. *Note*: Related dates are 11/25/55 — racial segregation banned on interstate trains and buses; 11/24/1869 — the American Woman Suffrage Association organized in Cleveland; 12/4/1833 — American Antislavery Society founded; 12/1/55 — Mrs. Rosa Parks, a black woman in Montgomery, Ala., arrested for sitting in the front of a bus; 1/10 — Human Rights Day; 12/15 — Bill of Rights Day.

30 Samuel Clemens (Mark Twain) born, 1835. Have a Mark Twain Odd Job Day. "The twain shall always meet — at the library!" If there are some cinderblock walls in a basement corridor that need painting, and you haven't the staff or time, organize a paint crew of patrons. If the lawn needs raking, have patrons bring rakes to the library and serve cider and doughnuts. Maybe it's time to take drapes for cleaning — get patrons to help out. Display selection of American books on the Mississippi — novels or journals.

December

3 Gilbert Stuart, first great American portrait painter, born, 1755. Have a display of portraits of local celebrities, or of teachers and librarians — done by children. Have a Polaroid Portrait day — they make great buttons if you get a pin-back button machine.

5 Christina Rossetti, sonnet writer, born, 1830. Make it the Week of the Sonnet, with readings aloud at lunch time for staff or public.

5 Walt Disney born, 1901. Do a week of cartoon movies, or make part of a group project where kids make their own cartoons by scratching on blank slides or 8-mm movie film.

8 James Thurber born, 1894. George Booth is the *New Yorker* cartoonist known for cats and dogs nowadays, but before him, Thurber's dogs were the cat's meow for years. Make white cardboard dummyboard cutouts of Thurberian dogs, about 2' high, with easel backs, and set them around the library — near Thurber books, books on cartooning, back issues of the *New Yorker*, dog care books.

8 John Lennon killed, 1980. Play Beatles music, have a capable and entertaining person do readings from Lennon's most entertaining *In His Own Write* and *A Spaniard in the Works*.

9 Noah Webster founded the *American Minerva*, NYC, 1793. First American newspaper that lasted. Your library's newspaper services and range of periodicals; books on journalism, journalism as a career — with a talk by working professionals for young or second career people.

10 Melvil Dewey born, 1851. Simplified spelling; phonetics; basics in library history and/or usage; lesson in cataloguing, arranging books, retrieving via computer.

10 Alfred Nobel, founder of the Nobel Prizes, died, 1896. Do display or program on some selected subject of the Prizes, and the winners.

10 United Nations Human Rights Day. The UN Declaration of Human Rights adopted, 1948. It seems fitting that the Nobel Peace Prize is awarded on this day.

Hanukkah — the Jewish Festival of Lights. With cooperation of local synagogues, do a display on meaning and customs of Hanukkah. Do dual display on this and on St. Lucia's Day, the 13th, another candlelit festival.

12 French novelist Gustave Flaubert born, 1821. Present booklist of "realist" novels of last 100 years. Have a novelist answer questions after reading selections for a work in progress.

16 Ludwig van Beethoven born, 1770. Have a recital or recorded concert of his music. Do a display of old or new musical instruments, or of sheet music you lend.

18 Renowned English clown, Joseph Grimaldi, born, 1779. Have fun — let any who want to, dress as clowns for the day. Hire a clown; do clown makeup on children; exhibit clown paintings and prints borrowed from community members. Get a pair of mimes to encourage passersby to come into the library.

19 *Poor Richard's Almanac* by Benjamin Franklin first published, 1732. Do up flyer using some of Franklin's witty and wise remarks, or adapt them specifically for a library fundraiser: "A learned blockhead is a greater blockhead than an ignorant one" (1734). "The heart of a fool is in his mouth, but the mouth of a wise man is in his heart" (1733). "The ancients tell us what is best; but we must learn of the moderns what is fittest" (1738). "Genius without Education is like Silver in the Mine" (1750). Do a "Penny Saved Penny Earned" display on investments or "Consumer Reports."

22 A coelacanth fish, thought by scientists to be extinct for last 65 million years, caught by fishermen off South African coast, 1938. Do a fossil display, or one on ocean exploration, or Jules Verne's books. Have children write a skit about a fisherman in the year 65,001,986 catching a snail darter.

25 Christmas Day. Do display of the symbols and customs of the "religious" Christmas and the "secular" Christmas. If Christmas and Hanukkah come close together, do dual display.

25 Nurse Clara Barton born, 1821. Nursing greats.

25 Cab Calloway, great jazz man, born, 1907.

25 The character of Sherlock Holmes first appeared in print, 1887, in *Beeton's Christmas Journal*.

30 Stephen Leacock, Canadian humorist and poet, born, 1869. Light verse books; Canadian humorists.

Selected Bibliography

The broad variety of old and new books listed below will help you plan and sustain a longterm program of displays, publicity events, and public relations. I strongly believe that if you approach a book of plans or ideas with the Zen "don't know" mind (meaning that you don't know what you'll find, but are open to every stimulus) you will find at least as many ideas lurking in your own mind as are to be found in the book.

Publicity & Public Relations

Barber, Peggy, ed. *68 Great Ideas: The Library Awareness Handbook.* Chicago: ALA, 1982. Softcover (SC), 66pp., illus. A lively potpourri of concisely outlined ideas for PR, fund-raising, publicity, cooperative programming, special events, advertising, etc. One valuable aspect: these ideas have all been implemented and a review of the contributing library's success with each idea is included. Recommended.

Eastman, Ann Heidbreder, and Roger H. Parent. *Great Library Promotion Ideas: [John Cotton Dana] Library Public Relations Award Winners and Notables 1984.* Chicago: ALA, 1984. SC, 77pp. (unpaginated), illus. This juried award has existed for forty years; the 1984 jury decided to identify isolated PR ideas of high quality from among all entries (which reflect a library's year-long overall effort). The 40 chosen are presented here, in $8\frac{1}{2} \times 11$ double column large-print format, about 1000 words each.

Edsall, Marian S. *Library Promotion Handbook.* Phoenix, AZ: Oryx Press, 1980. Hardcover (HC), 244pp., illus. Too long but full of information. Needed a *Reader's Digest* editor! But valuable concepts for creating an image, using the media to your advantage, raising funds, promoting special services. Good bibliography. Recommended.

Garvey, Mona. *Library Public Relations. A Practical Handbook.* New York: H.W. Wilson Co., 1980. HC, 160pp., illus. Handsomely produced and well-rounded book by author of two books I've not seen (*Library Displays*, and *Teaching Displays: Their Purpose, Construction and Use*). "Look at your library" carefully to determine marketing approaches, and decide on some programs and displays. An example of the practical but imaginative approach, here dealing with fines (in a school library), is "... begin the school year by mailing parents coupons good for 25¢ off on their children's fines." Obviously a book with wide application. Recommended.

Kohn, Rita, and Krysta Tepper. *You Can Do It: A PR Skills Manual for Librarians.* Metuchen, NJ: Scarecrow Press, 1981. SC, 232pp., illus. A practical guide to assessing PR needs and capabilities, then implementing them using a multi-media approach, i.e. signage, programs, outreach, graphics, etc. Recommended.

Manley, Will. *Snowballs in the Bookdrop: Talking It Over with Your Library's Community.* Hamden, CT: Shoe String Press, 1982. SC, 202pp. On developing rapport with the community, especially by doing a weekly newspaper column. Recommended.

O'Brien, Richard. *Publicity. How to Get It.* New York: Barnes & Noble Books/Harper & Row, 1977 (1978). SC, 176pp. Simplified, though not too much so, outline of publicity campaigning as an art—useful for libraries, but pitched to a slightly different audience.

Schwarz, Ted. *The Successful Promoter. 100 Surefire Ideas for Selling Yourself, Your Product, Your Organization.* Chicago: Contemporary Books, 1976. SC, 223pp. While much of it deals with the individual's desire for fame/fortune, libraries are made up of individuals and this may be a good real world tack to take for library PR. Two especially good chapters for us are the ones on window display, and one on "using newsletters."

Sherman, Steve. *ABC's of Library Promotion.* Metuchen, NJ: Scarecrow Press, 1971. HC, 182pp. Specifically for us, and full of vital ideas and tips. Particularly useful for the chapter "Evaluation of Your PR Program." Over and over, in all these books, the idea of assessment is stressed. An appendix, "Potpourri of Useful Facts and Figures," should be taken by each reader and updated and expanded to suit our times. These facts—concerning number of books published, the average person's interest in books, facts about early or historic libraries—are useful in placing promotion materials and press releases, and for annual reports. Recommended.

Tedone, David. *Practical Publicity. How to Boost Any Cause.* Harvard, MA: Harvard Common Press, 1982. HC & SC, 179pp., illus. Bibliography. Meant for volunteer, part-time publicists with limited budgets and time—sound familiar? Ideas for press release-writing, using radio spots, doing a newsletter, grass-roots canvassing, holding panel discussions and seminars, etc. Highly recommended.

Yale, David R. *The Publicity Handbook*. New York: Bantam Books, 1982. SC, 300pp. A terrific book "essential for civic groups, non-profit organizations, small businesses" as it says on the cover. Step-by-step procedures, with background reasoning, forecasting, dealing with the media, spotting newsworthy events — or creating them, writing press releases, radio spots, etc. Lengthy directory of useful services and sources. Highly recommended.

Activity Related

Bernstein, Bonnie. *Day by Day. 300 Calendar-Related Activities, Crafts, and Bulletin Board Ideas for the Elementary Grades*. Belmont, CA: Pitman Learning, 1980. SC, 234pp., illus. September to June scope; I've never understood why it's assumed all school activities cease in summer. But a good number of versatile ideas useable in libraries for adults as well as children. Readers of *Learning Magazine*, a useful Pitman publication, contributed many ideas. Unfortunately, some ideas are insensitive to animals, and while I may be more sensitive than some people to this, I think an important consideration before any display or program is put on is "How might this be construed as insensitive ... to minorities or animals?"

California Association of School Librarians. *Library Skills: A Handbook for Teachers and Librarians*. Belmont, CA: Fearon Publishers, 1958, 1973. SC, 88pp., illus. Projects-cum-games for K–2, 3–4 grades, 4–6 grades, and 3rd grade and up. To encourage loving and using the library.

Chase, William D., and Helen M. Chase. *Chase's Annual Events*. Chicago: Contemporary Books; annual since the late 1950s. SC, approx. 200pp. This belongs with your dictionary and Bartlett's. A must for planning special events, and available in the fall preceding the year it chronicles.

Frew, Andrew W. *Frew's Daily Archive: A Calendar of Commemorations*. Jefferson, NC: McFarland, 1984. HC, 384pp., several indexes. This will be useful as a display ideas calendar, particularly for the more off-beat interests. Contains over 4,500 events, more than 2,300 birthdates, and over 1,300 commemorations: something on every day of the year for practically any interest group.

Marshall, Karen K. *Back to Books. 200 Library Activities to Encourage Reading*. Jefferson, NC: McFarland, 1983. SC, 144pp., illus. Imaginative games, projects and classroom activities, with actual titles, authors, facts. Recommended.

Newmann, Dana. *The* New *Teacher's Almanack. Practical Ideas for Every*

Day of the School Year. West Nyack, NY: Center for Applied Research in Education, 1980. HC, 381pp., illus. September–June with events, days and ways to celebrate, crafts, experiments, riddles, bulletin boards, and an unusual appendix of recipes — for art materials as well as "classroom cookery." Interesting.

Preslan, Kristina, and Cecelia Mestas (illustrator). *Group Crafts for Teachers and Librarians on Limited Budgets.* Littleton, CO: Libraries Unlimited, 1980. SC, 105pp., illus. A book definitely focused on K–3, though with some wider application. 45 crafts — with one sample, total program consisting of story, song, discussion questions and craft, that shows how to place the other 44 in context. Thoughtful and thorough. Recommended.

Robotham, John S., and Lydia FaFleur. *Library Programs. How to Select, Plan and Produce Them,* 2nd ed. Metuchen, NJ: Scarecrow Press, 1981. HC, 352pp., illus. Bibliography. Important, rarely treated subject, developed here with full explanations of types of programs and what groups they appeal to, how to select programs and produce them without fuss, do publicity. Includes sample lists and programs. Highly recommended, because a regular schedule of well-planned and diverse programs helps publicize and humanize the library, making it seem as accessible as it really is.

Vinyard, Gayle. *Super Treasury of 300+ Activities, Games, Arts and Crafts.* Jefferson, NC: McFarland, 1984. SC, 238pp., illus. A broad range of immediate start-up activities to keep hands busy and minds at work. Good for rainy-day and other periods when librarians find themselves supervising children and young adults — materials are all mostly already "available": the key to this book is virtually no preparation time is needed.

Display & Bulletin Boards

Bowers, Melvyn K. *Easy Bulletin Boards for the School Library.* New York: Scarecrow Press, 1966. HC, 106pp., illus. Minimal text and technique explanation, but many designs are oddly charming. So simple that they've become less dated than many more complex ideas.

Buckley, Jim. *The Drama of Display. Visual Merchandising and Its Techniques.* New York: Pellegrini & Cudahy, 1953. HC, 227pp., illus. Dated in look, but full of professional tips and techniques — many shown in plan form — for the dynamics of focal points, lighting, etc. Marvelous chapter called "Improvisation" that is an imagination-booster for anyone who'd like to expand the pool from which displays are created. Recommended.

Burke, Kenneth, and Julie Kranhold. *Language Arts Ideas for Bulletin Boards*. Belmont, CA: Fearon Publishers, 1976. SC, 74pp., illus. For school teachers but with some applicable ideas for general libraries. To make displays, you'd need to add The Object of the Display, so that a book, service or event can be spotlighted. Teaching bulletin boards, to my mind, only do half the job.

Canoles, Marion L. *The Creative Copycat*. Littleton, CO: Libraries Unlimited, 1982. HC, 265pp., illus. 220 ideas, mostly for schools, most useful for its philosophy that display ideas are cheap — they're everywhere, lying in wait in magazine pictures, trash cans, boutique windows and other places.

_____. *The Creative Copycat II*. Littleton, CO: Libraries Unlimited, 1985. HC, 202pp., illus. An outgrowth of the above, this second volume offers nearly 150 more bulletin board display ideas.

Coplan, Kate. *Effective Library Exhibits. How to Prepare and Promote Good Displays*. New York: Oceana, 1958. HC, 127pp., illus. The appearance is dated, but there are many practical and well-described techniques for making displays. One rule of thumb in applying any of these ideas to today's needs: simplify even more and use the somewhat amateurish perfect symmetry sparingly.

_____. *Poster Ideas and Bulletin Board Techniques: For Libraries and Schools*, 2nd ed. New York: Oceana Publications, 1981. HC, 248pp., illus., some in color. A book by an eminent force in library display in Baltimore's Enoch Pratt Library, where she started doing displays, in an ad-hoc, make-do way in 1927! Interesting ideas, scores of them, showing simple techniques. Recommended.

Franklin, Linda Campbell. *Library Display Ideas*. Jefferson, NC: McFarland, 1980. HC & SC, 244pp., illus. About 110 displays, bulletin boards, bookmarks, flyers, etc., with complete how-to and materials lists. (None of the contents are repeated in the present work.)

_____. "Show Forth: A Newsletter of Display, Public Relations and Publicity Ideas for Librarians." A periodical, now ceased. (Jefferson, NC: McFarland, 1982–1984.) 8pp. each, illus. Sets of back issues still available in limited numbers. About ten ideas are incorporated into this book.

Goldman, Judith, with commentary by Gene Moore. *Windows at Tiffany's; The Art of Gene Moore*. New York: Harry N. Abrams, 1980. HC, 224pp., illus., many color. Scores of beautifully photographed windows, primarily at Tiffany's, the work of the genius of display, with text and commentary on designs. Inspiring for its many insights into the psychology, as well as the potential and purpose of window display. Much better than shopping inside Tiffany's! Highly recommended.

Koskey, Thomas Arthur. *How to Make and Use Flannel Boards: A Handbook for Teachers*. Belmont, CA: Fearon Publishers, 1961. SC, 24pp., illus. Small but fully-packed. Concise and widely applicable how-to. You provide the subjects to be treated.

Mauger, Emily M. *Modern Display Techniques*. New York: Fairchild Publications, 1964. HC, 127pp., illus. Store merchandising, but these days who cares? A professional and profitable approach; though it's 20 years old, it seems very up to date. Hundreds of "suggested copy" items listed in the back, many surprisingly useable for libraries. Recommended.

Randall, Reino, and Edward C. Haines. *Bulletin Boards and Display*. Worcester, MA: Davis Publishers, 1961, 1970. SC, 72pp., illus. Especially good for walk-through displays, using screens and dividers, not utilized enough in libraries. Lettering, and some craft techniques too.

Ruby, Doris, and Grant Ruby. *Bulletin Boards for the Middle Grades*. Belmont, CA: Fearon-Pitman, 1964. SC, 42pp., illus. Some ideas useful for attracting children to the library.

Talmadge, R.H. *Point of Sale Display*. London & New York: Studio Publications, 1958. HC, 96pp., illus. Here's an approach not widely understood in libraries, whereby many useable surfaces—on tables, counters, file cabinets, desks, bookcases and catalog cases—are left empty or decorated with stacks of flyers and stubby pencils. The ideas here, of course, are for powder and shampoo and salves, but are unbelievably suitable for books. If you can get a copy of this book, do it! Highly recommended.

"Visual Merchandising & Store Design." Monthly periodical. (Cincinnati, OH: Signs of the Times Publishing Co.) For retail stores, but with so much art and imagination that even libraries, without much display money or talent, can gain some expertise and a more professional look. Also good for sources of display materials. ST Publications puts out a goodly number of display-related books too.

Wallick, Clair H. *Looking for Ideas? A Display Manual for Libraries and Bookstores*. Metuchen, NJ: Scarecrow Press, 1970. HC, 104pp., illus. Each display idea represented with a photo, plus a description of what's used in it and why. Dated designs, but most are reworkable.

Graphics, Lettering, Signage

Adair, Ian. *Papercrafts*. London: David & Charles; New York: Arco Pub. Co., 1975, 1977. HC, 80pp., illus., some color. Many projects and 3-D objects of paper. Useful in making props for case and window displays.

Booth-Clibborn, Edward, and Daniele Baroni. *The Language of Graphics*.

New York: Harry N. Abrams, Inc., 1979. HC, 320pp., 1000+ illus. Rich and stimulating book dealing with communication and graphics as they relate to sociology, strategy, environment, publicity, objects ... plus an historic view and an interesting bibliography. Useful.

Cheatham, Frank R.; Jane Hart Cheatham, and Sheryl A. Haler. *Design Concepts and Applications*. Englewood Cliffs, NJ: Prentice-Hall, 1983. SC, 243pp., illus. Essentially a textbook for design students, this book has good illustrations from a wide variety of sources, each chosen for a design lesson. Generally readable commentary, useful to help build a strong conceptual foundation for display and graphics work. Not essential, but useful.

Coffin, Harry B. *Layout File for Printers and Advertisers: Design, Layout and Sales Ideas for Designers, Sellers or Buyers of Printing*. New York: Moore Pub. Co., 1957. SC, 65pp., illus. Reprint from *American Printer*, January 1952–August 1954. An "idea-starter" with many layouts and sketches for booklets, reports, announcements, folders, posters and more. Densely packed with ideas; so sound and classic that after 30 years only a tiny proportion seem dated. Recommended.

Cross, Peter R., ed., and Ruth E. Stiehl. *CON-TACT®. Classroom Graphics with CON-TACT® Brand Vinyl*. Belmont, CA: Fearon-Pitman Pub., 1978. SC, 92pp., illus. Not handsome, but some excellent ideas for using self-stick, transparent, colored or patterned vinyl. Other brands could be used. Not just for classrooms, but with wide application for walls, floors, posters, bulletin boards, etc., for libraries.

Kince, Eli. *Visual Puns in Design: The Pun Used As a Communication Tool*. New York: Watson-Guptill, 1982. HC, 168pp., illus. It's still debatable: is in fact the bun a low form of wheat? Certainly most people indulge, sometimes unconsciously. Puns are always capable of getting attention, and a visual pun or joke is a more sophisticated and subtle tool for display use. Recommended.

Lancaster, John. *Lettering Techniques*. New York: Arco, 1980, 1982. SC, 144pp., illus. A great lettering/graphic arts book that is, at the same time, both an artistic and historic overview of styles (including 16th century illuminations and Hong Kong signs), and a real how-to showing every kind of lettering technique, from typewriters to rubber stamps, doodling to pictograms. Many applicable to novices or amateurs.

Mallery, Mary S., and Ralph E. DeVore. *A Sign System for Libraries*. Chicago: ALA, 1982. SC, 33pp., illus. Useful as a working checklist. It is a system, just one, to adapt or adopt.

"Print: America's Graphic Design Magazine." Annual periodical. (New York: RC Publications.) Excellent reproduction of hundreds of fine designs used for brochures, print campaigns, posters, etc., useful to library display people as a source of ideas for visual images, unusual typefaces, the development of logos, etc. Recommended.

White, Jan V. *Graphic Idea Notebook: Inventive Techniques for Designing Printed Pages*. New York: Watson-Guptill, 1980. HC, 192pp., illus. A fine, varied scrapbook in effect, with one to 10 ideas per page that would be aids in designing flyers, brochures, bulletin boards, and certain elements of window and case displays. Highly recommended.

_____. *Mastering Graphics. Design and Production Made Easy*. New York: R.R. Bowker, 1983. SC, 180pp., illus. Marvelously clear, short course for creating good graphic layouts, using pictures, creating borders, directing viewers' gazes, etc. Make better posters, newsletters, annual reports, publicity flyers, etc. Highly recommended.

Materials, Supplies & Supplementary Materials

This list is tied to the displays in this book, but should be supplemented by the listing in the author's earlier book, *Library Display Ideas* (McFarland, 1980).

There are also some supplementary materials of interest to you, but which have not been discussed in the main body of the book.

Foam Boards

Semi-rigid sandwiches of cardboard and plastic foam, in various thicknesses, foam boards can be cut into sturdy free-standing props or displays, or used for creating temporary exhibition screens, etc. You can find some kind of foam board at most art supply stores, or write the manufacturers below for distribution information:

Fome-Cor ST and Fome Cor. Monsanto Engineered Products Division, 800 N. Lindbergh Blvd., St. Louis, MO 63167.

Gatorfoam. International Paper Company, Uniwood Division, POB 5380, Statesville, NC 28677.

Artcor. Amoco Foam Products Company, 2100 Powers Ferry Rd., Atlanta, GA 30099.

Prime-Foam-X. Primex Plastics Corp., ICC Industries Inc., 1 Raritan Rd., Oakland, NJ 07436.

Hooks

Selfix hooks, with their own adhesive, Selfix, Inc. 4501 W. 47th Street, Chicago, IL 60632.

Ceil-Clip. Ceil-Clip Co., 168 E. Mountain Road, Waterbury, CT 06706.

Plastic Films, Etc.

Window Skin. Printek, Div. of Anderberg-Lund Printing, 6989 Oxford St., St. Louis Park, MN 55426.
Pantone. Tint overlays, color coated papers, etc. Mfd. by Letraset, Inc. Available at all art supply stores.
Con-Tact Vinyl. Comark Plastics Division, United Merchants & Manufacturers, Inc., 3601 Hempstead Turnpike, Levittown, LI, NY 11756.
Write-on Plastic Sheets. Highsmith Co., Inc., POB 25, Fort Atkinson, WI 53538.

Posters

Bonnie Slotnick Designs. Set of 6 law library posters to "enforce library regulations with humor" — no eating signs, one requesting quiet, one on theft and vandalism. A 7th poster is for general libraries — a "reshelve your books poster." All printed 11 × 17 on 65# cover stock. $10 each, ppd. Bonnie Slotnick, 68 W. 10th, Apt. 33, NYC, NY 10011.

Animated Displays

By this is meant the electrically-motivated figures seen at Christmas in shop windows, or occasionally in shoe repair windows or carpentry/woodwork suppliers. The range of possible figures, and the movements they make, is wonderful, and is something to seriously consider for use as a permanent library "mascot" or fixture in the story-telling room, or anywhere else. All kinds of animals and human figures, in many sizes, available — reasonably — and some can be dressed yourself.

David Hamberger Inc.. 410 Hicks Street, Brooklyn, NY 11201.

Organizations

Reading is FUNdamental, Inc. L'Enfant 2500, Smithsonian Institution, Washington, DC 20560.

Openers Promotion Kits. Openers, American Library Association, 50 E. Huron St., Chicago, IL 60611.

Adopt-a-Grandparent. Westside Independent Service to the Elderly, 1320 Santa Monica Mall, Santa Monica, CA 90401.

Literacy Volunteers of America. 404 Oak St., Syracuse, NY 13203.

Benjamin Franklin Stamp Club Headquarters. U.S.P.S., Washington, DC 20260.

Directory

"Visual Merchandising & Store Design Buyers' Guide," published by the magazine of the same name, Signs of the Times Publishing Company, 407 Gilbert Avenue, Cincinnati, OH 45202. For the ideas in the monthly magazine, and the list of manufacturers and trade names for display products, you should subscribe to this magazine.

Index

Most numbers in parentheses are dates in the calendar
section. Most entries in italics are display titles.